MATH Expressions
Common Core

Dr. Karen C. Fuson

GRADE
2

Volume 2

This material is based upon work supported by the
National Science Foundation
under Grant Numbers
ESI-9816320, REC-9806020, and RED-935373.

Any opinions, findings, and conclusions, or recommendations expressed in this material
are those of the author and do not necessarily reflect the views of the National Science Foundation.

VOLUME 2 CONTENTS

UNIT 4 Subtract 2-Digit Numbers

BIG IDEA 1	Totals of Mixed Coins and Bills

BIG IDEA 2	Multidigit Subtraction Strategies

* This lesson consists only of activities from the Teacher Edition.

VOLUME 2 CONTENTS *(continued)*

UNIT 5 Time, Graphs, and Word Problems

© Houghton Mifflin Harcourt Publishing Company

VOLUME 2 CONTENTS *(continued)*

UNIT 7 Arrays, Equal Shares, and Adding or Subtracting Lengths

***** This lesson consists only of activities from the Teacher Edition.

BIG IDEA 2   Relate Addition and Subtraction to Length

Student Resources

Dear Family:

In this unit, your child will find the value of various coin combinations. Children will also combine different coins to equal one dollar.

25¢ + 25¢ + 10¢ + 10¢ + 10¢ + 10¢ + 10¢ = 100¢

Then your child will count both dollars and coins.

Say: $1.00 $1.25 $1.35 $1.40

You can help at home by providing opportunities for your child to practice counting money. Begin with amounts less than $1.00.

Please call if you have any questions or concerns. Thank you for helping your child to learn mathematics.

Sincerely,
Your child's teacher

COMMON CORE   Unit 4 includes the Common Core Standards for Mathematical Content for Operations and Algebraic Thinking, 2.OA.1, 2.OA.2; Number and Operations in Base Ten, 2.NBT.4, 2.NBT.5, 2.NBT.6, 2.NBT.7, 2.NBT.8, 2.NBT.9; Measurement and Data, 2.MD.8; and all Mathematical Practices.

Estimada familia:

En esta unidad su niño va a hallar el valor de diversas combinaciones de monedas. Los niños también combinarán diferentes monedas para igualar el valor de un dólar.

25¢ + 25¢ + 10¢ + 10¢ + 10¢ + 10¢ + 10¢ = 100¢

Luego, su niño contará billetes de dólares y monedas.

Se dice:　　　　$1.00　　　　$1.25　　$1.35　　$1.40

Usted puede ayudar a su niño proporcionándole en casa oportunidades de practicar contando dinero. Empiece con cantidades menores que $1.00.

Si tiene alguna duda o algún comentario, por favor comuníquese conmigo. Gracias por ayudar a su niño a aprender matemáticas.

Atentamente,
El maestro de su niño

COMMON CORE

La Unidad 4 incluye los Common Core Standards for Mathematical Content for Operations and Algebraic Thinking, 2.OA.1, 2.OA.2; Number and Operations in Base Ten, 2.NBT.4, 2.NBT.5, 2.NBT.6, 2.NBT.7, 2.NBT.8, 2.NBT.9; Measurement and Data, 2.MD.8; and all Mathematical Practices.

Cut on dashed lines.

© Houghton Mifflin Harcourt Publishing Company

Coin Cards

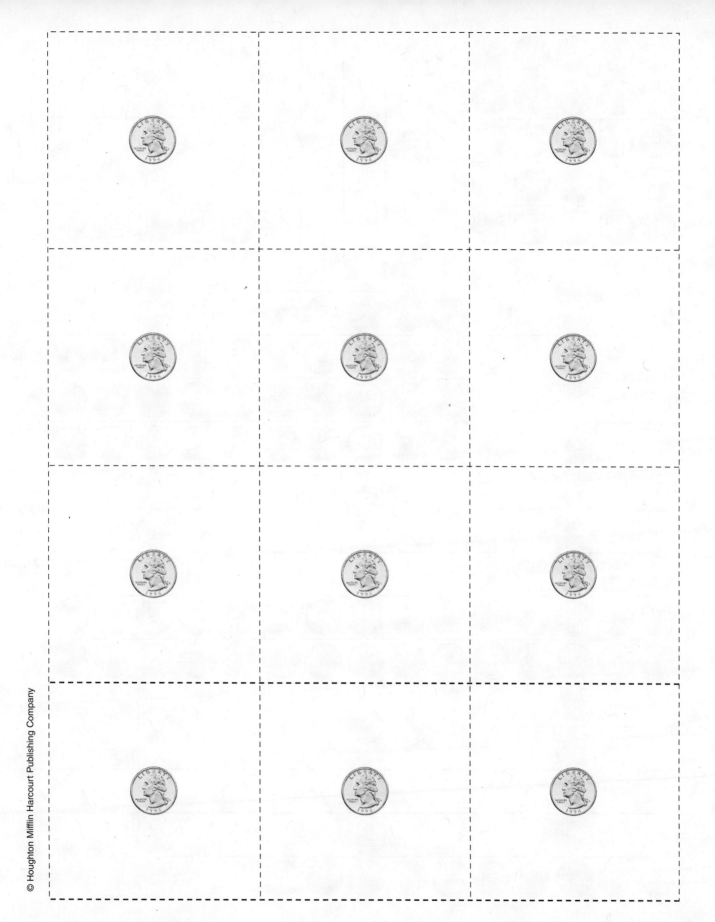

Cut on dashed lines.

Quarter Squares (front) **163**

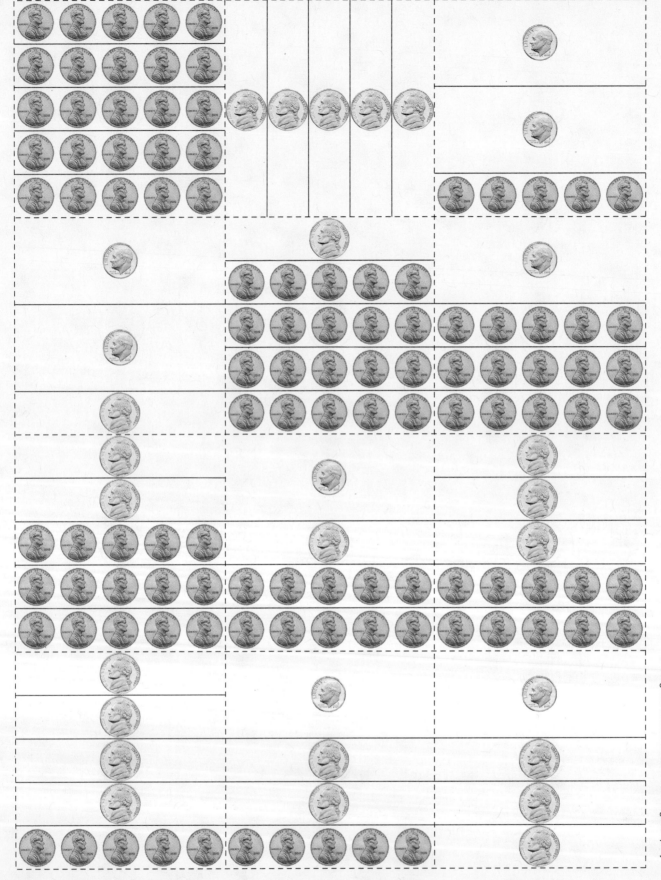

Cut only on dashed lines.

Quarter Squares (back)

Cut on dashed lines.

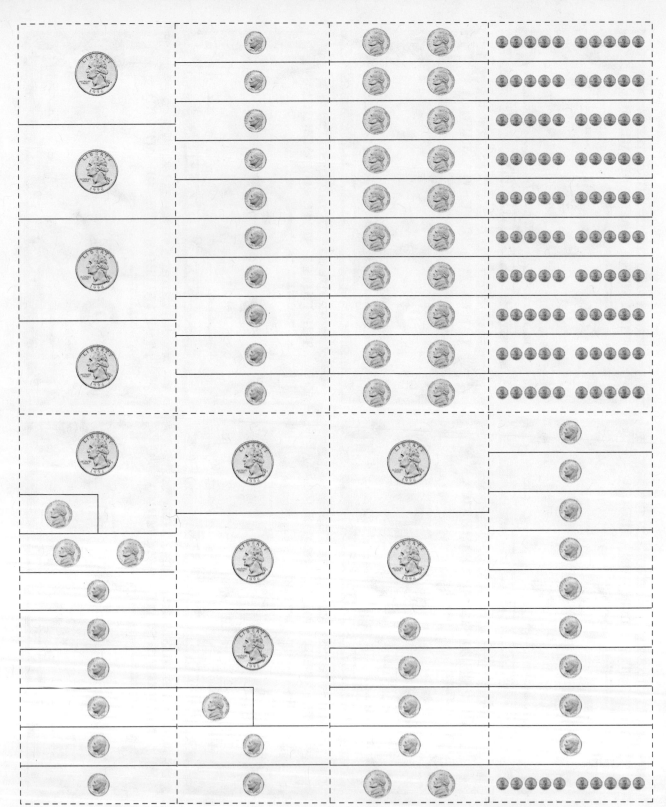

Cut only on dashed lines.

Dollar Equivalents (back)

Name _____

▶ Count Coins and Bills

Under each picture, write the total amount of money so far.
Then write the total using $. The first one is done for you.

1.   25¢   25¢   10¢   5¢

   25¢   50¢   60¢   65¢ $ 0 . 6 5

                                                  total

2.   25¢   10¢   10¢   1¢   1¢

_____ _____ _____ _____ _____ $ ___.___

                                                  total

3.   100¢   25¢   5¢   5¢

_____ _____ _____ _____ $ ___.___

                                                  total

4. Bo has 1 dollar, 2 quarters, 1 dime, 4 nickels, and 3 pennies.
    Draw ⬜100 s, (25) s, (10) s, (5) s, and (1) s.

Write the total amount of money. $ ___.___

                                                  total

▶ What's the Error?

100¢   1¢   1¢

$ 1 . 2 ___

I wrote the total. Did I make a mistake?

5. Show Puzzled Penguin how you would find the total amount of money. Under each picture, write the total amount so far.

100¢   1¢   1¢

_____ _____ _____ $ ___.___
total

▶ More Practice Writing Totals

Under each picture, write the total amount of money so far.
Then write the total using $.

6.   100¢   5¢

$ ___.___
total

7.   100¢   5¢   1¢   1¢

$ ___.___
total

VOCABULARY
ungroup

▶ Word Problems: Ungrouping 100

When you subtract, you can use the following drawings to help you **ungroup**.

Use Dollars to Ungroup	Use Quick Tens to Ungroup
100¢ 1 0 0 (• • • • • • • • • •) 0 10 1̸ 0̸ 0 (• • • • • • • • • | ∶) 9 0 1̸0̸ 10 1̸ 0̸ 0	

Solve the word problems.

Show your work.

1. The baker bakes 100 loaves of bread. He sells 73 loaves. How many loaves are left?

   ☐ _____

   label

2. Jim has 100 flowers in his garden. He gives 35 of them away. How many flowers are left in Jim's garden?

   ☐ _____

   label

3. The letter carrier has 100 letters in her bag. She delivers 52 letters. How many letters are left in her bag?

   ☐ _____

   label

▶ Subtract from 100

Solve. Rewrite the hundred or make a drawing.

4. $100 - 62 =$ ☐

5. $100 - 83 =$ ☐

6. $100 - 79 =$ ☐

7. $100 - 54 =$ ☐

Addends and Subtraction

Dear Family:

In this program, children learn these two methods for 2-digit subtraction. However, children may use any method that they understand, can explain, and can do fairly quickly.

Expanded Method	Ungroup First Method
Step 1 "Expand" each number to show that it is made up of tens and ones. $$64 = 60 + 4$$ $$-28 = 20 + 8$$ **Step 2** Check to see if there are enough ones to subtract from. If not, ungroup a ten into 10 ones and add it to the existing ones. $$64 = \cancel{60} \overset{50}{} + \cancel{4}\,\overset{14}{}$$ $$-28 = 20 + 8$$ **Step 3** Subtract to find the answer. Children may subtract from left to right or from right to left. $$64 = \cancel{60}\overset{50}{} + \cancel{4}\,\overset{14}{}$$ $$-28 = 20 + 8$$ $$\overline{\quad 30 + 6 = 36 \quad}$$	**Step 1** Check to see if there are enough ones to subtract from. If not, ungroup by opening up one of the 6 tens in 64 to be 10 ones. 4 ones plus these new 10 ones make 14 ones. We draw a magnifying glass around the top number to help children focus on the regrouping.  **Step 2** Subtract to find the answer. Children may subtract from left to right or from right to left. 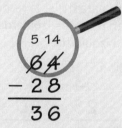

In explaining any method they use, children are expected to use "tens and ones" language. This shows that they understand they are subtracting 2 tens from 5 tens (not 2 from 5) and 8 ones from 14 ones.

Please call if you have any questions or comments.

Sincerely,
Your child's teacher

COMMON CORE   Unit 4 includes the Common Core Standards for Mathematical Content for Operations and Algebraic Thinking, 2.OA.1, 2.OA.2; Number and Operations in Base Ten, 2.NBT.4, 2.NBT.5, 2.NBT.6, 2.NBT.7, 2.NBT.8, 2.NBT.9; Measurement and Data, 2.MD.8; and all Mathematical Practices.

© Houghton Mifflin Harcourt Publishing Company

Estimada familia:

En este programa, los niños aprenden estos dos métodos para restar con números de 2 dígitos. Sin embargo, pueden usar cualquier método que comprendan, puedan explicar y puedan hacer relativamente rápido.

Método extendido	Método de desagrupar primero
Paso 1 "Extender" cada número para mostrar que consta de decenas y unidades. $$64 = 60 + 4$$ $$-28 = 20 + 8$$ **Paso 2** Observar si hay suficientes unidades para restar. Si no las hay, desagrupar una decena para formar 10 unidades y sumarla a las unidades existentes. $$\begin{array}{r}50 \quad 14\\64 = \cancel{60} + \cancel{4}\\-28 = 20 + 8\end{array}$$ **Paso 3** Restar para hallar la respuesta. Los niños pueden restar de izquierda a derecha o de derecha a izquierda. $$\begin{array}{r}50 \quad 14\\64 = \cancel{60} + \cancel{4}\\-28 = 20 + 8\\\hline 30 + 6 = 36\end{array}$$	**Paso 1** Observar si hay suficientes unidades para restar. Si no las hay, desagrupar una de las 6 decenas en 64 para obtener 10 unidades. 4 unidades más las 10 unidades nuevas son 14 unidades. Dibujamos una lupa alrededor del número superior para ayudar a los niños a concentrarse en desagrupar.  **Paso 2** Restar para hallar la respuesta. Los niños pueden restar de izquierda a derecha o de derecha a izquierda. 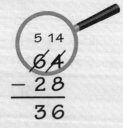

Cuando los niños expliquen el método que usan, deben hacerlo usando un lenguaje relacionado con "decenas y unidades". Esto demuestra que comprenden que están restando 2 decenas de 5 decenas (no 2 de 5) y 8 unidades de 14 unidades.

Si tiene alguna duda o algún comentario, por favor comuníquese conmigo.

Atentamente,
El maestro de su niño

La Unidad 4 incluye los Common Core Standards for Mathematical Content for Operations and Algebraic Thinking, 2.OA.1, 2.OA.2; Number and Operations in Base Ten, 2.NBT.4, 2.NBT.5, 2.NBT.6, 2.NBT.7, 2.NBT.8, 2.NBT.9; Measurement and Data, 2.MD.8; and all Mathematical Practices.

VOCABULARY
Expanded Method

►Explain the Expanded Method

Mr. Green likes this method. Explain what he does.		
Step 1	**Step 2**	**Step 3**

Step 1

$$64 = 60 + 4$$
$$- 28 = 20 + 8$$

‖‖‖ ‖ ○○○○

Step 2

$$64 = \overset{50}{\cancel{60}} + \overset{14}{\cancel{4}}$$
$$- 28 = 20 + 8$$

⊞⊞⊞⊞⊞
⊞⊞⊞⊞⊞

‖‖‖‖ ✳ ○○○○

Step 3

$$64 = \overset{50}{\cancel{60}} + \overset{14}{\cancel{4}}$$
$$- 28 = 20 + 8$$
$$\overline{30 + 6 = 36}$$

⊞⊞⊞⊞⊞
⊞⊞⊞⊞⊞

卅‖‖‖ ✳ ○○○○

►Try the Expanded Method

Show your work numerically and with a proof drawing.

1. $\begin{array}{r} 42 \\ -19 \\ \hline \end{array}$

2. $\begin{array}{r} 75 \\ -46 \\ \hline \end{array}$

3. $\begin{array}{r} 81 \\ -37 \\ \hline \end{array}$

VOCABULARY
Ungroup First Method

▶ Explain the Ungroup First Method

Mrs. Green likes this method. Explain what she does.

Step 1	Step 2	Step 3
$\begin{array}{r} 64 \\ -28 \\ \hline \end{array}$	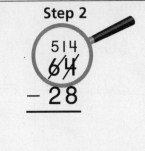 $\begin{array}{r} 514 \\ \cancel{6}\cancel{4} \\ -28 \\ \hline \end{array}$	$\begin{array}{r} 514 \\ \cancel{6}\cancel{4} \\ -28 \\ \hline 36 \end{array}$

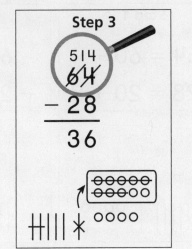

▶ Try the Ungroup First Method

Show your work numerically and with a proof drawing.

4. 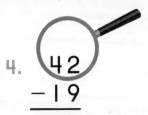 $\begin{array}{r} 42 \\ -19 \\ \hline \end{array}$

5.  $\begin{array}{r} 75 \\ -46 \\ \hline \end{array}$

6.  $\begin{array}{r} 81 \\ -37 \\ \hline \end{array}$

Two Methods of Subtraction

VOCABULARY
difference

▶ Solve and Discuss

Subtract to find the **difference.**

1. $\begin{array}{r} 75 \\ -47 \\ \hline \end{array}$

2. $\begin{array}{r} 54 \\ -18 \\ \hline \end{array}$

3. $\begin{array}{r} 94 \\ -36 \\ \hline \end{array}$

4. $\begin{array}{r} 66 \\ -34 \\ \hline \end{array}$

5. $\begin{array}{r} 85 \\ -58 \\ \hline \end{array}$

6. $\begin{array}{r} 89 \\ -69 \\ \hline \end{array}$

7. $\begin{array}{r} 82 \\ -59 \\ \hline \end{array}$

8. $\begin{array}{r} 97 \\ -78 \\ \hline \end{array}$

9. $\begin{array}{r} 65 \\ -28 \\ \hline \end{array}$

10. $\begin{array}{r} 78 \\ -19 \\ \hline \end{array}$

11. $\begin{array}{r} 53 \\ -26 \\ \hline \end{array}$

12. $\begin{array}{r} 91 \\ -46 \\ \hline \end{array}$

Name _____

▶ What's the Error?

$$
\begin{array}{r}
\overset{13}{8\,\cancel{3}} \\
-\ 5\,5 \\
\hline
3\,8
\end{array}
$$

Did I make a mistake?

13. Show Puzzled Penguin how you would subtract.
Draw a proof diagram to check your work.

$$
\begin{array}{r}
8\,3 \\
-\ 5\,5 \\
\hline
\end{array}
$$

▶ PATH to FLUENCY Add and Subtract Within 20

Add.

14. $9 + 4 =$ ☐   15. $6 + 5 =$ ☐   16. $3 + 4 =$ ☐

17. $\begin{array}{r} 8 \\ +\ 7 \\ \hline \end{array}$ 18. $\begin{array}{r} 4 \\ +\ 8 \\ \hline \end{array}$ 19. $\begin{array}{r} 5 \\ +\ 9 \\ \hline \end{array}$

Subtract.

20. $17 - 8 =$ ☐   21. $13 - 5 =$ ☐   22. $14 - 7 =$ ☐

23. $\begin{array}{r} 9 \\ -\ 6 \\ \hline \end{array}$ 24. $\begin{array}{r} 1\,5 \\ -\ 6 \\ \hline \end{array}$ 25. $\begin{array}{r} 1\,6 \\ -\ 8 \\ \hline \end{array}$

Practice and Explain a Method

►Explain Ungrouping 200

Use this drawing to explain why $200 = 100 + 90 + 10$.

► Review Both Methods

Expanded Method

$$
\begin{array}{r}
200 \\
-\ 68 \\
\hline
\end{array}
=
\begin{array}{c}
\overset{100}{200} + \overset{\overset{90}{100}}{\cancel{}}\ 0 + \overset{10}{\cancel{0}} \\
60\ +\ 8
\end{array}
\ \text{or}\
\begin{array}{c}
\overset{100}{200} + \overset{90}{\cancel{0}} + \overset{10}{\cancel{0}}
\end{array}
$$

$$100\ +\ 30\ +\ 2 = 132$$

Ungroup First Method

Ungroup in two steps.　or　**Ungroup all at once.**

Step 1. Ungroup
I hundred to
make 10 tens.

Step 2. Ungroup I ten
to make 10 ones.

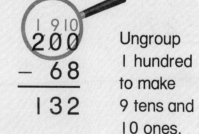

or

Ungroup
I hundred
to make
9 tens and
10 ones.

$$200 = 100 + 90 + 10$$

Explain how ungrouping and subtraction work.

Relate the steps used in these methods to the drawing at the top of the page.

▶ Practice the Ungroup First Method

Use the Ungroup First Method to find each difference.

1. $\begin{array}{r} 2\,0\,0 \\ -\ \ 8\,7 \\ \hline \end{array}$

2. $\begin{array}{r} 2\,0\,0 \\ -\ \ 8\,9 \\ \hline \end{array}$

3. $\begin{array}{r} 2\,0\,0 \\ -\ \ 4\,6 \\ \hline \end{array}$

4. $\begin{array}{r} 2\,0\,0 \\ -\ \ 3\,8 \\ \hline \end{array}$

5. $\begin{array}{r} 2\,0\,0 \\ -\ \ 2\,7 \\ \hline \end{array}$

6. $\begin{array}{r} 2\,0\,0 \\ -\ \ 8\,2 \\ \hline \end{array}$

Subtract from 200

▶ Decide When to Ungroup

Decide if you need to ungroup. Then subtract.

1.   1 3 4
   − 7 8
   ‾‾‾‾‾‾‾

   Did you ungroup a ten to
   get more ones? _____
   Did you ungroup a hundred
   to get more tens? _____

2.   1 3 4
   − 7 3
   ‾‾‾‾‾‾‾

   Did you ungroup a ten to get
   more ones? _____
   Did you ungroup a hundred
   to get more tens? _____

3.   1 5 8
   − 3 7
   ‾‾‾‾‾‾‾

   Did you ungroup a ten to get
   more ones? _____
   Did you ungroup a hundred
   to get more tens? _____

4.   1 3 8
   − 5 9
   ‾‾‾‾‾‾‾

   Did you ungroup a ten to get
   more ones? _____
   Did you ungroup a hundred
   to get more tens? _____

5.   1 4 6
   − 5 7
   ‾‾‾‾‾‾‾

   Did you ungroup a ten to get
   more ones? _____
   Did you ungroup a hundred
   to get more tens? _____

6.   1 4 6
   − 3 5
   ‾‾‾‾‾‾‾

   Did you ungroup a ten to get
   more ones? _____
   Did you ungroup a hundred
   to get more tens? _____

▶ Decide When to Ungroup (continued)

Decide if you need to ungroup. Then subtract.

7.　167
　　− 42
　　─────

Did you ungroup a ten to get more ones? _____
Did you ungroup a hundred to get more tens? _____

8.　148
　　− 39
　　─────

Did you ungroup a ten to get more ones? _____
Did you ungroup a hundred to get more tens? _____

9.　124
　　− 86
　　─────

Did you ungroup a ten to get more ones? _____
Did you ungroup a hundred to get more tens? _____

10.　150
　　− 27
　　─────

Did you ungroup a ten to get more ones? _____
Did you ungroup a hundred to get more tens? _____

11.　139
　　− 75
　　─────

Did you ungroup a ten to get more ones? _____
Did you ungroup a hundred to get more tens? _____

12.　172
　　− 68
　　─────

Did you ungroup a ten to get more ones? _____
Did you ungroup a hundred to get more tens? _____

　　　　　Ungroup from the Left or from the Right

▶ Subtract with Zeros

Decide if you need to ungroup. Then subtract.

1.
```
  1 0 8
-   4 6
```

2.
```
  1 0 3
-   6 5
```

3.
```
  1 5 0
-   7 9
```

4.
```
  1 0 2
-   8 3
```

5.
```
  1 6 0
-   9 2
```

6.
```
  1 0 7
-   6 1
```

7.
```
  1 0 6
-   3 8
```

8.
```
  1 7 0
-   4 0
```

9.
```
  1 8 0
-   9 3
```

10.
```
  1 4 0
-   5 7
```

11.
```
  1 5 0
-   8 4
```

12.
```
  1 0 6
-   4 3
```

▶ Solve and Discuss

Decide if you need to ungroup. Then subtract.

13.
```
  1 0 6
-   8 1
```

14.
```
  1 1 0
-   1 8
```

15.
```
  1 9 0
-   7 2
```

16.
```
  1 0 7
-   3 8
```

17.
```
  1 3 0
-   2 2
```

18.
```
  1 2 0
-   6 3
```

Solve each word problem. Make a
math drawing if you need more help.

Show your work.

19. Mr. Gordon sells cars. He wants to sell 109 cars
this month. So far he has sold 34 cars. How many
more cars does he need to sell?

```
┌─────┐
│     │  _____
└─────┘
        label
```

20. Mrs. Dash grilled 110 burgers for the
school picnic. 79 were eaten. How many
burgers are left?

```
┌─────┐
│     │  _____
└─────┘
        label
```

Zero in the Ones or Tens Place

▶ Act it Out

First, see how much money you have. Then decide what to buy. Pay for the item. Then write how much money you have left.

Yard Sale

Cork Board	Toy Rabbit	Toy Guitar	Perfume	Knit Cap
78¢	84¢	75¢	89¢	99¢

1. I have 162¢ in my pocket.

   I bought the _____.

   $$
   \begin{array}{r}
   1\ 6\ 2¢ \\
   -\ \ \ \ \ ¢ \\
   \hline
   \end{array}
   $$

   I have _____ ¢ left.

2. I have 143¢ in my pocket.

   I bought the _____.

   $$
   \begin{array}{r}
   1\ 4\ 3¢ \\
   -\ \ \ \ \ ¢ \\
   \hline
   \end{array}
   $$

   I have _____ ¢ left.

3. I have 154¢ in my pocket.

   I bought the _____.

   $$
   \begin{array}{r}
   1\ 5\ 4¢ \\
   -\ \ \ \ \ ¢ \\
   \hline
   \end{array}
   $$

   I have _____ ¢ left.

4. I have 126¢ in my pocket.

   I bought the _____.

   $$
   \begin{array}{r}
   1\ 2\ 6¢ \\
   -\ \ \ \ \ ¢ \\
   \hline
   \end{array}
   $$

   I have _____ ¢ left.

Name _____

▶ Use a Dollar Sign

Write the money amount. The first one is done for you.

5. 134¢ = __1__ dollar __3__ dimes __4__ pennies = $ __1__ . __3__ __4__

6. 76¢ = _____ dollars _____ dimes _____ pennies = $ ____ . ____ ____

7. 179¢ = _____ dollar _____ dimes _____ pennies = $ ____ . ____ ____

8. 58¢ = _____ dollars _____ dimes _____ pennies = $ ____ . ____ ____

Find the difference. Use play money to help you
ungroup, if you wish.

9.	10.	11.
$1.44 − .23	$1.25 − .95	$1.63 − .95
12.	13.	14.
$1.58 − .45	$1.36 − .75	$1.92 − .95

Model Subtraction with Money

▶ **PATH to FLUENCY Subtract Within 100**

Subtract.

1.   65
    −16
    ____

2.   58
    −37
    ____

3.   20
    −14
    ____

4.   74
    −23
    ____

5.   19
    −17
    ____

6.   50
    −13
    ____

7.   87
    −30
    ____

8.   91
    −45
    ____

9.   31
    − 9
    ____

10. 97
    −79
    ____

11. 20
    − 7
    ____

12. 46
    −36
    ____

▶ PATH to FLUENCY **Subtract Within 100 (continued)**

Subtract.

13.
```
  1 0 0
-   4 8
```

14.
```
  6 7
- 3 1
```

15.
```
  5 5
- 1 6
```

16.
```
  8 3
-   8
```

17.
```
  4 0
- 2 6
```

18.
```
  1 9
- 1 1
```

19.
```
  1 4
- 1 1
```

20.
```
  2 5
- 1 2
```

21.
```
  1 0 0
-   1 9
```

22.
```
  9 4
- 7 6
```

23.
```
  2 0
-   8
```

24.
```
  7 7
- 2 4
```

Fluency: Subtraction Within 100

▶ **PATH to FLUENCY** *Ungroup Challenge*

Work in 👥. Lay out Secret Code Cards like this.

¹⁰ **1 0**	⁶⁰ **6 0**	¹ **1**	⁶ **6**
²⁰ **2 0**	⁷⁰ **7 0**	² **2**	⁷ **7**
³⁰ **3 0**	⁸⁰ **8 0**	³ **3**	⁸ **8**
⁴⁰ **4 0**	⁹⁰ **9 0**	⁴ **4**	⁹ **9**
⁵⁰ **5 0**		⁵ **5**	

1. 🧍 Use Secret Code Cards to help you make a 2-digit subtraction (top number less than 100).

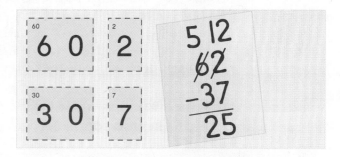

2. Make another 2-digit subtraction.

- Use the same tens cards.

- If 🧍 *ungrouped a ten,* use ones cards that *do not need more ones.*

- If 🧍 *did not ungroup a ten,* use ones cards that *need more ones.*

Activity continues on next page.

► ⟨ PATH to FLUENCY ⟩ *Ungroup Challenge* (continued)

2. 👥 Work together to check your work.
Correct any errors.

3. Put the Secret Code Cards back. Switch
roles and repeat. Continue until time is up.

*To play as a game and compete with another pair,
use the **Scoring Rules** below.*

Scoring Rules

for

Ungroup Challenge

• Trade papers with another pair.

• Put a ✓ next to each correct answer.
  Put an X next to each incorrect answer.

• Give 1 point for each ✓.
  Subtract 3 points for each X.

• The pair with more points wins.

▶ Addition and Subtraction Word Problems

Draw a Math Mountain to solve each word problem. Show how you add or subtract.

Show your work.

1. Teresa has 45 blocks. Then she finds 29 more under the couch. How many blocks does Teresa have now?

☐ _____
label

2. Krina's class makes 163 masks. They hang 96 of the masks in the library. How many masks do they have left?

☐ _____
label

3. There are 12 girls and 8 boys in the library. How many children are in the library altogether?

☐ _____
label

4. The school store has 90 glue sticks. Then 52 glue sticks are sold. How many glue sticks are left?

☐ _____
label

▶ Addition and Subtraction Word Problems (continued)

Draw a Math Mountain to solve each word problem. Show how you add or subtract.

Show your work.

---

5. Sam has 47 marbles. Hank has 53 marbles. How many marbles do they have in all?

☐ _____
   label

---

6. Mrs. Snap has 42 pencils. She gives 29 pencils to her students and puts the rest in a box. How many pencils does she put in the box?

☐ _____
   label

---

7. At the park, Pam collects 25 leaves. Eighteen are oak leaves and the rest are maple leaves. How many are maple leaves?

☐ _____
   label

---

8. Mr. Vazquez has 64 paintbrushes. He gives the art teacher 8 paintbrushes. How many paintbrushes does Mr. Vazquez have left?

☐ _____
   label

▶ Find Equations for Math Mountains

1. Write all of the equations for 83, 59, and 24.

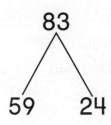

$59 + 24 = 83$

_____

_____

_____

$83 = 59 + 24$

_____

_____

_____

2. Write all of the equations for 142, 96, and 46.

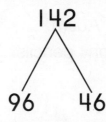

$96 + 46 = 142$

_____

_____

_____

$142 = 96 + 46$

_____

_____

_____

► Word Problem Practice: Addition and Subtraction Within 20

Make a drawing. Write an equation. Solve.

Show your work.

---

3. There are 7 children at the lunch table.
   Some more children sit down. Then
   there are 11 children at the table. How
   many children sit down?

   □ _____
                label

---

4. Some leaves are on the ground. The children
   pick up 9 leaves. Then there are 3 leaves on
   the ground. How many leaves were on the
   ground at the start?

   □ _____
                label

---

5. Teri has 5 more pencils than Adam.
   Adam has 6 pencils. How many pencils
   does Teri have?

   □ _____
                label

---

6. Stevie has 8 more stickers than Ari.
   Stevie has 13 stickers. How many stickers
   does Ari have?

   □ _____
                label

Equations with Greater Numbers

► **PATH to FLUENCY** **Practice Addition and Subtraction Within 100**

Add or subtract. Watch the sign!

1. $\begin{array}{r} 91 \\ -63 \\ \hline \end{array}$

2. $\begin{array}{r} 36 \\ +\ 9 \\ \hline \end{array}$

3. $\begin{array}{r} 100 \\ -\ 74 \\ \hline \end{array}$

4. $\begin{array}{r} 45 \\ +39 \\ \hline \end{array}$

5. $\begin{array}{r} 64 \\ -23 \\ \hline \end{array}$

6. $\begin{array}{r} 33 \\ +66 \\ \hline \end{array}$

7. $\begin{array}{r} 20 \\ -\ 4 \\ \hline \end{array}$

8. $\begin{array}{r} 34 \\ +38 \\ \hline \end{array}$

9. $\begin{array}{r} 52 \\ -38 \\ \hline \end{array}$

10. $\begin{array}{r} 43 \\ +57 \\ \hline \end{array}$

11. $\begin{array}{r} 96 \\ -78 \\ \hline \end{array}$

12. $\begin{array}{r} 13 \\ +79 \\ \hline \end{array}$

▶ **Solve and Discuss**

Solve each word problem.

Show your work.

13. Tamyra bakes 48 muffins on Monday. On Tuesday
she bakes 24 muffins. How many muffins does she
bake during those two days?

☐ _____
      label

14. Mrs. Jennings gets 75 new books for the class
library. She places 37 of them on the shelf. How
many new books are left to place on the shelf?

☐ _____
      label

15. Isaac has 64 toy cars. Twenty-five of them are in
a box. How many cars are not in the box?

☐ _____
      label

16. In June, Sarah reads 18 books. In July,
she reads 35 books. How many books
does she read in June and July?

☐ _____
      label

Practice Addition and Subtraction

▶ **Introduce the Juice Bar**

Grapefruit Juice 11¢	Red Apple Juice 41¢	Lemon Juice 20¢	Pear Juice 22¢
Green Apple Juice 25¢	Peach Juice 40¢	Orange Juice 18¢	Cantaloupe Juice 10¢
Pineapple Juice 47¢	Raspberry Juice 33¢	Banana Juice 39¢	Watermelon Juice 15¢
Grape Juice 50¢	Celery Juice 36¢	Tomato Juice 30¢	Carrot Juice 29¢

▶ Continue Buying and Selling

Choose two juice samples from the Juice Bar you would like to mix together. Find the total cost. Then find the change from one dollar.

1. I pick _____

and _____.

Juice 1 price: _____ ¢

Juice 2 price: + _____ ¢

Total: _____

100¢ − _____ = _____

My change is _____ ¢.

2. I pick _____

and _____.

Juice 1 price: _____ ¢

Juice 2 price: + _____ ¢

Total: _____

100¢ − _____ = _____

My change is _____ ¢.

3. I pick _____

and _____.

Juice 1 price: _____ ¢

Juice 2 price: + _____ ¢

Total: _____

100¢ − _____ = _____

My change is _____ ¢.

4. I pick _____

and _____.

Juice 1 price: _____ ¢

Juice 2 price: + _____ ¢

Total: _____

100¢ − _____ = _____

My change is _____ ¢.

Buy and Sell with One Dollar

▶ Practice the Adding Up Method

Add up to solve each word problem.

Show your work.

___

1. Doug has 62 baseball cards. After he goes shopping today, he will have 86 baseball cards. How many baseball cards is Doug going to buy?

   ☐ _____

   label

___

2. Myra has 87 dollars. She buys some gifts. Then she has 68 dollars. How much money does Myra spend on gifts?

   ☐ _____

   label

___

3. There are 15 apples in a basket. Some more apples are put in. Now there are 23 apples in the basket. How many apples are put in?

   ☐ _____

   label

___

4. Mr. Azim finds 113 golf balls. After he gives some to Carey, he has 54 golf balls left. How many golf balls does Mr. Azim give to Carey?

   ☐ _____

   label

▶ Practice the Adding Up Method (continued)

Add up to solve each word problem.

Show your work.

5. Frank has 27 sheets of green paper. He uses some to wrap presents. Then he has 18 sheets of green paper. How many sheets does he use?

☐ _____
  label

6. There are 25 bikes at a store. Then some more bikes are brought to the store. Now there are 48 bikes at the store. How many bikes are brought to the store?

☐ _____
  label

7. There are 95 pieces of popcorn in a bag. Jennifer eats some of the pieces. Now there are 52 pieces in the bag. How many pieces does Jennifer eat?

☐ _____
  label

8. In a package of stickers, there are 45 red stickers and some blue stickers. There are 100 stickers in all. How many stickers are blue?

☐ _____
  label

Word Problems with Unknown Addends

Name _____

▶**Practice the Adding Up Method**

Solve each word problem.   Show your work.

1. Justin reads 27 comics. Trina reads some
   comics. In all, they read 86 comics. How
   many comics does Trina read?

   ☐ _____
        label

2. Maya and Phillip draw 73 pictures. Maya draws 38 of
   the pictures. How many pictures does Phillip draw?

   ☐ _____
        label

3. There are 82 birds in the zoo. The zoo gets
   some more birds. Now they have 100 birds.
   How many birds does the zoo get?

   ☐ _____
        label

4. Mrs. Clark has 94 pens. She gives some
   pens to her friends. Now she has 75 pens.
   How many pens does Mrs. Clark give away?

   ☐ _____
        label

▶ Practice the Adding Up Method (continued)

Add up to solve each word problem.   Show your work.

5. Austin has 54 crayons. His sister gives him
   some more crayons. Now he has 82 crayons.
   How many crayons does his sister give him?

   ☐ _____
         label

6. In Robert's classroom, there are 39 books on a red shelf.
   There are some books on a green shelf. There are 78 books
   on the two shelves. How many books are on the green shelf?

   ☐ _____
         label

▶ (PATH to FLUENCY) Add and Subtract Within 100

Add.

7.   22
  + 30

8.   17
  + 3

9.   51
  + 34

10.   86
  + 9

Subtract.

11.   100
  − 68

12.   92
  − 15

13.   83
  − 77

14.   54
  − 29

More Word Problems with Unknown Addends

►Solve Complex Word Problems

Write an equation. Solve the problem.

1. Marian has a collection of toy cars. She gives 28 cars to her brother Simon. Marian has 57 cars left. How many cars did she have to begin with?

_____
label

2. In September, Mr. Shaw planted some tulip bulbs. In October, he planted 35 more bulbs. Altogether he planted 81 bulbs. How many bulbs did he plant in September?

_____
label

3. Mrs. Lyle has a collection of 19 mugs. She buys some more. Now she has 34 mugs. How many mugs did Mrs. Lyle buy?

_____
label

4. Tarik picks 41 flowers. He gives some of the flowers to his aunt. He has 24 flowers left. How many flowers did Tarik give to his aunt ?

_____
label

▶ Solve Complex Word Problems (continued)

Write an equation. Solve the problem.

5. Frank has some markers. He buys 15 more markers. Now he has 62 markers. How many markers did Frank have to begin with?

☐ _____
label

6. Kiki has 74 stickers. She gives some stickers to her friends. Now she has 29 stickers. How many stickers did Kiki give to her friends?

☐ _____
label

7. Miss Harrod has a jar with some paperclips in it. She gives 53 paperclips to the science teacher. There are 37 paperclips left in the jar. How many paperclips were in the jar before?

☐ _____
label

8. Josef has 59 sports cards. His friend Tara gives him some more cards. Now Josef has 78 sports cards. How many cards did Tara give him?

☐ _____
label

Start Unknown Problems

Name _____

▶ Solve *Compare* Word Problems

Draw comparison bars and write an equation
to solve each problem.

1. Tia has 65 stamps. Stan has
29 stamps. How many more
stamps does Tia have than Stan?

☐ _____
    label

2. Dora has 27 fewer grapes than
Jerry. Jerry has 72 grapes. How
many grapes does Dora have?

☐ _____
    label

3. Lila has 34 snow globes in her
collection, which is 18 fewer
than her friend Betty has.
How many snow globes does
Betty have in her collection?

☐ _____
    label

4. One year the Ricos planted 97
flowers. This was 29 more than
the Smiths planted. How many
flowers did the Smiths plant?

☐ _____
    label

▶ Solve *Compare* Word Problems (continued)

Draw comparison bars and write an equation
to solve each problem.

5. Pippa has 48 more beads than
   Jeremy. Jeremy has 38 beads.
   How many beads does
   Pippa have?

6. In the classroom, there are
   25 fiction books and 64 nonfiction
   books. How many fewer fiction
   books than nonfiction books are
   in the classroom?

☐ _____
label

☐ _____
label

7. Boris has 16 more cherries than
   Solongo. Boris has 60 cherries.
   How many cherries does
   Solongo have?

8. Mrs. Karimi has 36 fewer
   crayons than Mr. Cabral.
   Mrs. Karimi has 57 crayons.
   How many crayons does
   Mr. Cabral have?

☐ _____
label

☐ _____
label

►Solve and Discuss

Make a drawing. Write an equation. Solve.

---

1. Maxine cuts out 48 squares to make a quilt.
   She needs 16 more squares to complete the quilt.
   How many squares will be in the quilt altogether?

   ☐ _____
        label

---

2. Mr. Adams buys 93 paper plates for a party.
   He buys 43 large plates. The rest are small.
   How many small plates does he buy?

   ☐ _____
        label

---

3. Chad collects stamps. He has 32 stamps. Loren gives
   him some more stamps. Now Chad has 51 stamps.
   How many stamps did Loren give Chad?

   ☐ _____
        label

---

4. Trina's team scores 56 points at the basketball game.
   This is 30 more points than the other team scores.
   How many points does the other team score?

   ☐ _____
        label

▶ Solve and Discuss (continued)

Make a drawing. Write an equation. Solve.

5. Maura gives 19 trading cards to Jim. Now she has 24 trading cards. How many trading cards did Maura have to start?

☐ _____
   label

6. Jamal has 63 toy cars. Luis has 24 fewer toy cars than Jamal. How many toy cars does Luis have?

☐ _____
   label

7. Anna has some red balloons and some blue balloons. Altogether she has 46 balloons. How many balloons of each color could she have?

☐ _____ and ☐ _____
   label   label

8. Jon has 71 stickers. Ken has 53 stickers. How many fewer stickers does Ken have than Jon?

☐ _____
   label

Mixed Word Problems

▶ Solve and Discuss (continued)

Make a drawing. Write an equation. Solve.

---

9. Amanda has 22 more color pencils than Troy. Troy has 38 color pencils. How many color pencils does Amanda have?

◻ _____
              label

---

10. Nicole is matching spoons and forks. She finds 36 spoons and 50 forks. How many more spoons does Nicole need to have the same number of spoons as forks?

◻ _____
              label

---

11. Kristi has some shells. Then she finds 24 more shells at the beach. Now Kristi has 100 shells. How many shells did she start with?

◻ _____
              label

---

12. Gabby has 84 beads. She uses some beads to make a necklace. Now she has 45 beads left. How many beads does Gabby use to make the necklace?

◻ _____
              label

Name _____

▶ What's the Error?

Sona has 63 balloons. That is 16 more balloons than Molly. How many balloons does Molly have?

$$63 + 16 = 79$$
Sona   more   Molly

Did I make a mistake?

13. Draw comparison bars to help Puzzled Penguin. Write an equation to solve the problem.

Molly has [ ] balloons.

▶ PATH to FLUENCY Add and Subtract Within 100

Add.

14.	15.	16.
34	13	49
+ 46	+ 78	+ 26

Subtract.

17.	18.	19.
95	61	60
− 38	− 28	− 33

Mixed Word Problems

▶ Solve Two-Step Problems

Think about the first-step question.
Then solve the problem.

1. A farmer has two crates of milk bottles for sale.
   Each crate has 24 bottles. He sells 35 bottles.
   How many bottles of milk are left?

   ☐ _____
   label

2. There are 26 children at the library. 12 are girls and
   the rest are boys. Then 7 more boys come to the
   library. How many boys are at the library now?

   ☐ _____
   label

3. Jeff has 2 boxes of crayons and 15 other
   crayons. Each box contains 36 crayons.
   How many crayons does Jeff have altogether?

   ☐ _____
   label

▶ Solve Two-Step Problems (continued)

Think about the first-step question.
Then solve the problem.

4. Whitney collects 18 cans for recycling. Tara collects 9 cans. Julia collects 12 more cans than Whitney and Tara collect together. How many cans does Julia collect?

☐ _____
        label

5. Margie has 17 balloons. Logan has 9 more balloons than Margie. Bonnie has 12 fewer balloons than Logan. How many balloons does Bonnie have?

☐ _____
        label

6. Mr. Tyson makes 75 rings to sell at a fair. He sells 16 rings on the first day. He sells some more on the second day. Now he has 22 rings left. How many rings did Mr. Tyson sell on the second day?

☐ _____
        label

▶ Solve Two-Step Problems

Think about the first-step question.
Then solve the problem.

1. Lin gets $38 for babysitting. She spends $12 on a present for her mother and puts the rest in a money jar. She then gives some money to her sister. Now she has $18. How many dollars did Lin give her sister?

☐ _____
     label

2. Russell has 28 marbles. Ridge has 12 fewer marbles than Russell. Natasha has as many marbles as Russell and Ridge together. How many marbles does Natasha have?

☐ _____
     label

3. Mr. Verdi is sewing costumes for the school play. He needs 26 blue buttons. He also needs 16 green buttons and 34 red buttons. How many buttons does Mr. Verdi need in all?

☐ _____
     label

▶ Solve Two-Step Problems (continued)

Think about the first-step question.
Then solve the problem.

4. Jolinda starts with 56 patches for her quilt. 25 are red
   and the rest are green. She adds some more green
   patches to the quilt. Now there are 36 green patches
   in her quilt. How many green patches does Jolinda
   add to the quilt?

   ☐ _____
   label

5. Gabe and Juan find 32 feathers. Mari and Kaila find
   12 more feathers than Gabe and Juan. If Mari finds
   19 feathers, how many feathers does Kaila find?

   ☐ _____
   label

6. Kyle plants 15 seeds in the first pot. He plants
   12 seeds in the second pot and 18 seeds in the third
   pot. The fourth pot is large. He plants as many seeds
   in the fourth pot as in all the other three pots. How
   many seeds does Kyle plant in the four pots altogether?

   ☐ _____
   label

More Two-Step Problems

►Math and Dinosaurs

The Stegosaurus was a large plant-eating dinosaur.
It had two rows of plates running along its back
and long spikes on its tail.

The feet of the Stegosaurus were short and wide.
The forefeet (the feet on the front legs) had
five short, wide toes with short hoof-like
tips. The rear feet had three short,
wide toes with hooves.

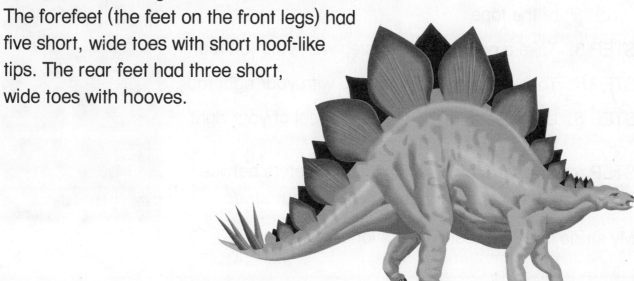

1. The rear foot of a Stegosaurus was about
   35 centimeters long. Use scissors and tape to make
   a paper strip that is 35 centimeters long. Write on the
   strip: *Foot of Stegosaurus.*

2. Now measure your own foot in centimeters.

   My foot is ☐ centimeters long.

   Make a paper strip that is the same length as your
   foot. Write on the strip: *My Foot.*

3. How much longer is the foot of the Stegosaurus than
   your foot?

   ☐ centimeters

© Houghton Mifflin Harcourt Publishing Company

▶ Measure Stride

4. Work with a partner to measure your *stride*.

STEP 1. Put a piece of tape on the floor.

STEP 2. Line up your right and left heels with the edge of the tape.

STEP 3. Take a normal walking step with your left foot.

STEP 4. Take a normal walking step with your right foot.

STEP 5. Use tape to mark where the heel of your right foot lands.

STEP 6. Measure the distance in centimeters between the two pieces of tape. This is your *stride*.

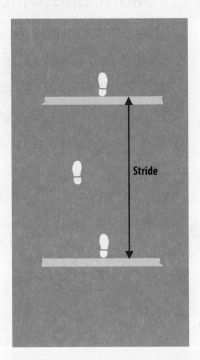

My stride is ⬜ centimeters long.

Make a paper strip that is the same length as your stride. Write on the strip: *My Stride.*

5. The stride of the Stegosaurus is measured using footprints from its right hind leg. Its stride was about 190 centimeters. Make a paper strip that is 190 centimeters long. Write on it: *Stride of Stegosaurus.*

6. How much longer is the stride of the Stegosaurus than your stride?

⬜ centimeters

7. Compare your stride with your partner's stride.

Who has the longer stride? _____

How much longer is it? ⬜ centimeters

Focus on Mathematical Practices

Subtract.

1.
$$
\begin{array}{r}
19 \\
-\ 5 \\
\hline
\end{array}
$$

2.
$$
\begin{array}{r}
20 \\
-\ 7 \\
\hline
\end{array}
$$

3.
$$
\begin{array}{r}
32 \\
-\ 8 \\
\hline
\end{array}
$$

4.
$$
\begin{array}{r}
63 \\
-\ 27 \\
\hline
\end{array}
$$

5.
$$
\begin{array}{r}
84 \\
-\ 19 \\
\hline
\end{array}
$$

6.
$$
\begin{array}{r}
92 \\
-\ 46 \\
\hline
\end{array}
$$

7.
$$
\begin{array}{r}
57 \\
-\ 25 \\
\hline
\end{array}
$$

Under each picture, write the total amount of money so far. Use ¢.
Then write the total using $.

8. 25¢   25¢   25¢   10¢   10¢   5¢   1¢

25¢   50¢   ___   ___   ___   ___   ___

$ ___ . ___
total

9. Faith has 2 dollars, 1 quarter, 3 dimes, 1 nickel, and 1 penny.
Draw ⬛100 s, Ⓐ25 s, Ⓐ10 s, Ⓐ5 s, and Ⓐ1 s. Write the total
amount of money.

$ ___ . ___
total

Subtract.

10.
$$\begin{array}{r} 100 \\ -\ 18 \\ \hline \end{array}$$

11.
$$\begin{array}{r} 200 \\ -\ 43 \\ \hline \end{array}$$

12.
$$\begin{array}{r} 179 \\ -\ 81 \\ \hline \end{array}$$

13.
$$\begin{array}{r} 198 \\ -\ 56 \\ \hline \end{array}$$

14.
$$\begin{array}{r} 130 \\ -\ 67 \\ \hline \end{array}$$

15.
$$\begin{array}{r} 104 \\ -\ 13 \\ \hline \end{array}$$

16.
$$\begin{array}{r} 156 \\ -\ 39 \\ \hline \end{array}$$

17.
$$\begin{array}{r} 143 \\ -\ 84 \\ \hline \end{array}$$

Solve.   Show your work.

18. Vince has 32 purple bicycles and some red
bicycles in his store. He has 67 bicycles
altogether. How many red bicycles does he have?

☐
_____
label

19. Bonita has 19 more raisins than Peter. Peter
has 25 raisins. How many does Bonita have?

☐
_____
label

20. There are 35 birds in the yard. Some more birds fly
into the yard. Now there are 77 birds. How many
birds fly into the yard?

☐
_____
label

21. Jeffrey buys paper cups for his party. He uses
46 paper cups at the party. There are 29 paper
cups left. How many paper cups did Jeffrey buy
for his party?

☐
_____
label

Solve.   Show your work.

22. Amy, Ben, and Cho bring apples to school.
Amy brings 25 apples. Ben brings 11 more
apples than Amy. Cho brings 16 fewer apples
than Ben. How many apples does Cho bring?

_____ _____
             label

23. Jackie, Corban, and Shaun play basketball on
the same team. During a game, Jackie scores
15 points, Corban scores 30 points, and Shaun
scores 21 points. How many points do they score
in all?

_____ _____
             label

24. Margo has 46 more marbles than Kyle. Margo has
72 marbles. How many marbles does Kyle have?

_____ _____
             label

25. **Extended Response** Explain all the steps you do
to subtract 59 from 78.

_____

_____

_____

Dear Family:

Your child is beginning a new unit on time.

You can help your child link the time concepts learned in school with the real world.

Together, look for clocks in your home. You might search for watches, alarm clocks, digital clocks, and clocks on appliances.

Talk about time throughout your family's day. For example, you can point to the clock during breakfast and say, "We usually eat breakfast at this time. It is 7:30 A.M."

In this unit, your child will learn to tell time to the hour, half hour, and five minutes. Your child will practice writing the time.

If you have any questions or comments, please call or write to me. Thank you.

Sincerely,
Your child's teacher

COMMON CORE Unit 5 includes the Common Core Standards for Mathematical Content for Operations and Algebraic Thinking, 2.OA.1, 2.OA.2; Number and Operations in Base Ten, 2.NBT.2, 2.NBT.5; Measurement and Data, 2.MD.7, 2.MD.10; Geometry, 2.G.3 and all Mathematical Practices.

Estimada familia:

Su niño está empezando una unidad donde aprenderá sobre la hora.

Usted puede ayudarlo a que conecte los conceptos relacionados con la hora que aprendió en la escuela, con el mundo real.

Busquen juntos relojes en la casa. Puede buscar relojes de pulsera, relojes con alarma, relojes digitales y relojes que estén en los electrodomésticos.

Durante un día en familia, hablen de la hora. Por ejemplo, puede señalar un reloj durante el desayuno y decir: "Generalmente desayunamos a esta hora. Son las 7:30 a.m."

En esta unidad su niño aprenderá a leer la hora en punto, la media hora y los cinco minutos para la hora. Su niño practicará cómo escribir la hora.

Si tiene alguna pregunta o algún comentario, por favor comuníquese conmigo. Gracias.

Atentamente,
El maestro de su niño

© Houghton Mifflin Harcourt Publishing Company

COMMON CORE

La Unidad 5 incluye los Common Core Standards for Mathematical Content for Operations and Algebraic Thinking, 2.OA.1, 2.OA.2; Number and Operations in Base Ten, 2.NBT.2, 2.NBT.5; Measurement and Data, 2.MD.7, 2.MD.10; Geometry, 2.G.3 and all Mathematical Practices.

Name _____

VOCABULARY
clock   minute hand
analog clock   hour hand

▶ Features of Clocks

Clocks are tools that we use to measure time.

1. Describe some clocks that you have seen.

_____

_____

_____

Place the missing numbers on the **analog clocks**.

2.

3.

4.

An analog clock has a long hand that is the **minute hand** and a short hand that is the **hour hand**.
Ring the hour hand on the clocks.

5.

6.

7.

Ring the minute hand on the clocks.

8.

9.

10.

VOCABULARY

A.M.

P.M.

► **Times of Daily Activities**

We use **A.M.** for the hours after 12:00 midnight and before 12:00 noon.
  9:00 A.M. is 9 o'clock in the morning.
We use **P.M.** for the hours after 12:00 noon and before 12:00 midnight.
  9:00 P.M. is 9 o'clock in the evening.

11. Complete the chart. For each time listed, write whether it is dark or light outside; whether it is morning, afternoon, or evening; and an activity you might be doing at that time.

Time	Sunlight	Part of the Day	Activity
4:00 A.M.	dark	morning	sleeping
12:30 P.M.			
9:00 P.M.			

For each activity, ring the most appropriate time.

12. brush your teeth in the morning

  1:30 P.M.   3:00 P.M.   7:30 A.M.

13. eat dinner at night

  5:00 A.M.   12:00 noon   6:00 P.M.

14. watch an afternoon movie

  3:00 A.M.   2:00 P.M.   6:00 P.M.

Name _____

► **Model a Clock**

Attach the clock hands using a prong fastener.

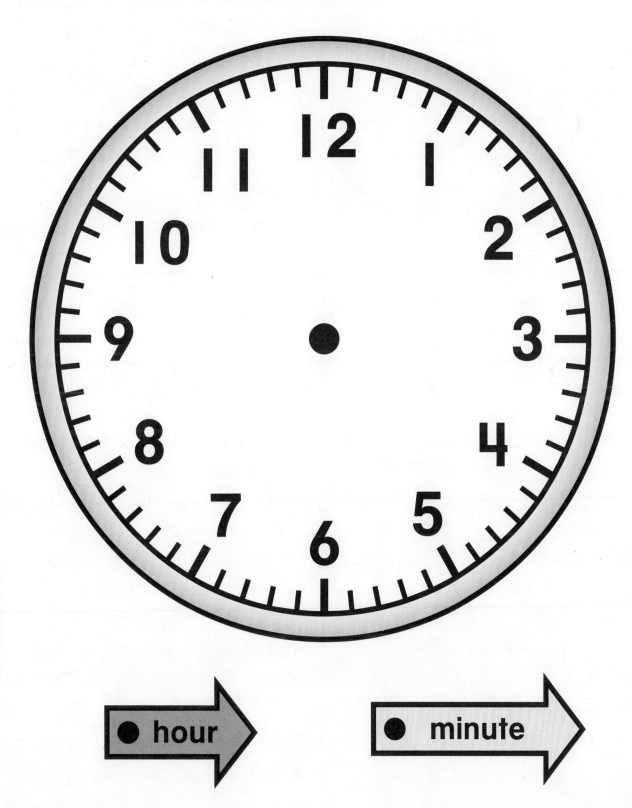

● hour ➤

● minute ➤

Paper Clock

VOCABULARY
digital clock

► Write Time

On a **digital clock**, the number on the left shows the hour, and the number on the right shows the minutes after the hour.

hour   minutes

Write the time in two different ways.

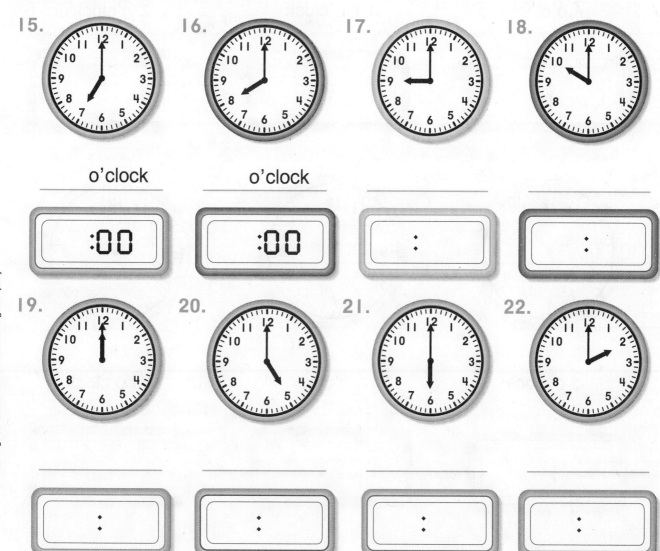

15.

o'clock

:00

16.

o'clock

:00

17.

:

18.

:

19.

:

20.

:

21.

:

22.

:

► **Draw Clock Hands**

Draw the hands on each analog clock, and write
the time on each digital clock below.

23.

7 o'clock

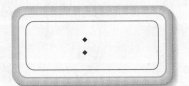

24.

11 o'clock

25.

2 o'clock

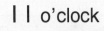

26.

3 o'clock

27.

5 o'clock

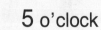

28.

10 o'clock

Hours and A.M. or P.M.

▶5-Minute Intervals

1. Count by 5s around the clock.

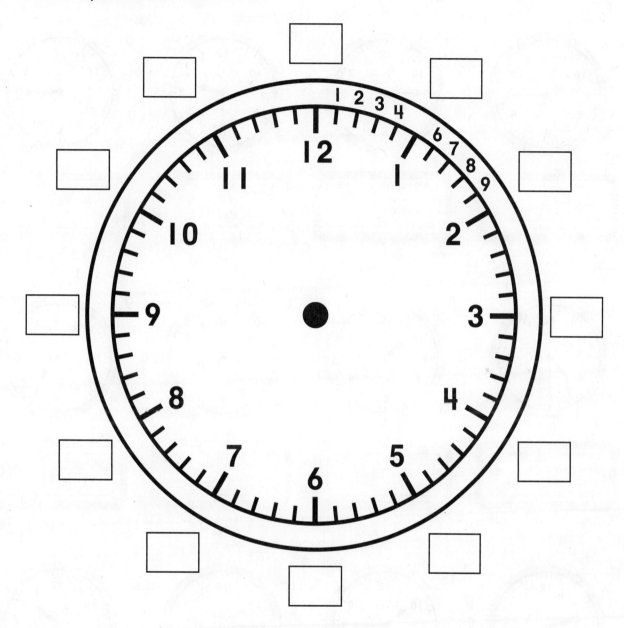

Name _____

▶ Read Time to 5 Minutes

Write the time on the digital clocks.

2.

3.

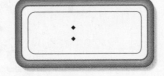

4.

5.

6.

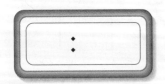

7.

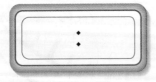

8.

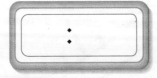

9.

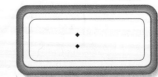

10.

11.

12.

13.

▶ Show Times to 5 Minutes

Draw hands on each clock to show the time.

14.

15.

16.

17.

18.

19.

20.

21.

22.

23.

24.

25.

▶ What's the Error?

Did I make a mistake?

26. What is the correct time?

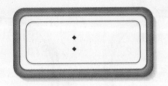

▶ A.M. or P.M.?

For each activity, ring the appropriate time.

27. picnic

5:30 A.M.
5:30 P.M.

28. school recess

10:00 A.M.
10:00 P.M.

29. afternoon snack

3:15 A.M.
3:15 P.M.

30. going to the playground

9:25 A.M.
9:25 P.M.

31. lunch

12:10 A.M.
12:10 P.M.

32. sunset

7:05 A.M.
7:05 P.M.

33. wake up

6:45 A.M.
6:45 P.M.

34. math class

8:30 A.M.
8:30 P.M.

Dear Family:

Your child is learning how to show information in various ways. In this unit, children will learn how to create and read picture graphs and bar graphs.

Picture Graph
Pennies

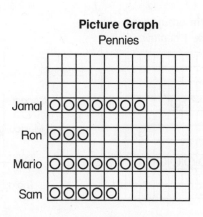

Bar Graph
Coins in My Collection

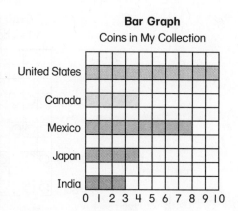

An important feature of *Math Expressions* is its emphasis on real world connections. Children will collect and represent data on graphs. They will also interpret the graph to answer questions about the data shown.

Children also explore the language of comparison by using such words as *same, more, less,* and *fewer.* The connection between pairs of terms is emphasized. For example: Carlos has 8 stickers. Maria has 3. Carlos has 5 *more* stickers than Maria. Maria has 5 *fewer* stickers than Carlos has.

Please call if you have any questions or concerns. Thank you for helping your child learn how to create, read, and interpret graphs.

Sincerely,
Your child's teacher

COMMON CORE Unit 5 includes the Common Core Standards for Mathematical Content for Operations and Algebraic Thinking, 2.OA.1, 2.OA.2; Number and Operations in Base Ten, 2.NBT.2, 2.NBT.5; Measurement and Data, 2.MD.7, 2.MD.10; Geometry, 2.G.3 and all Mathematical Practices.

Estimada familia:

Su niño está aprendiendo a mostrar información de varias maneras. En esta unidad los niños aprenderán a crear y a leer gráficas de dibujos y gráficas de barras.

Gráfica de dibujos
Monedas de 1 centavo

Gráfica de barras
Monedas de mi colección

Un aspecto importante de *Math Expressions* es su énfasis en las conexiones con situaciones de la vida cotidiana. Los niños reunirán datos y los representarán en gráficas. También interpretarán las gráficas para responder preguntas acerca de los datos que se muestran.

Los niños también estudiarán palabras que se usan para comparar, tales como *igual, mismo, más* y *menos*. Se hará énfasis en la conexión entre los pares de términos. Por ejemplo: Carlos tiene 8 adhesivos. María tiene 3. Carlos tiene 5 adhesivos *más* que María. María tiene 5 adhesivos *menos* que Carlos.

Si tiene alguna pregunta o algún comentario, por favor comuníquese conmigo. Gracias por ayudar a su niño a aprender cómo crear, leer e interpretar gráficas.

Atentamente,
El maestro de su niño

COMMON CORE   La Unidad 5 incluye los Common Core Standards for Mathematical Content for Operations and Algebraic Thinking, 2.OA.1, 2.OA.2; Number and Operations in Base Ten, 2.NBT.2, 2.NBT.5; Measurement and Data, 2.MD.7, 2.MD.10; Geometry, 2.G.3 and all Mathematical Practices.

► **Use Picture Graphs to Compare Amounts**

Read the **picture graph**.

Write the number. Ring *more* or *fewer*.

Number of Balloons	
Carla	🎈🎈🎈🎈🎈🎈🎈
Peter	🎈🎈🎈🎈
Hanna	🎈🎈🎈🎈

1. Carla has [ ] *more   fewer* balloons than Peter.

2. Hanna has [ ] *more   fewer* balloons than Carla.

Read the picture graph. Write the number.

Leaves Collected	
Amari	🍃🍃🍃🍃
Sam	🍃🍃🍃🍃🍃🍃🍃🍃
Marco	🍃🍃🍃🍃🍃🍃

3. Amari needs [ ] more leaves to have as many as Sam has.

4. If Sam gives away [ ] leaves, he will have as many leaves as Marco has.

▶Solve *Put Together/Take Apart* Problems

This picture graph shows the number of apples
Mrs. Reid bought at the store.

5. How many apples did Mrs. Reid
buy altogether?

☐ _____
　　　　　label

Apples Bought	
Red	🍎 🍎 🍎 🍎
Green	🍏 🍏
Yellow	🍎 🍎

6. There are 2 green apples, 1 yellow apple, and 1 red
apple in the bowl. The rest are in Mrs. Reid's bag.
How many apples are in the bag?

☐ _____
　　　　　label

This picture graph shows the number of
books that four children read.

7. Two children read 6 books altogether.
Who are the two children?

_____ and _____

Books Read	
Pablo	📕 📕 📕
Janis	📕 📕
Helen	📕
Ray	📕 📕 📕 📕

8. Two of the books the children read are about cars and
2 books are about trains. The rest of the books are about
animals. How many books are about animals?

☐ _____
　　　　　label

Read Picture Graphs

VOCABULARY
bar graph

► Make a Picture Graph

Title: _____

► Make a **Bar Graph**

Title: _____

Name _____

▶ **PATH to FLUENCY** **Add and Subtract Within 100**

Add.

1. $46 + 4 =$ _____   2. $3 + 39 =$ _____   3. $26 + 71 =$ _____

4. $\begin{array}{r} 56 \\ +36 \\ \hline \end{array}$ 5. $\begin{array}{r} 11 \\ +47 \\ \hline \end{array}$ 6. $\begin{array}{r} 36 \\ +53 \\ \hline \end{array}$ 7. $\begin{array}{r} 78 \\ +6 \\ \hline \end{array}$

8. $\begin{array}{r} 25 \\ +61 \\ \hline \end{array}$ 9. $\begin{array}{r} 18 \\ +60 \\ \hline \end{array}$ 10. $\begin{array}{r} 44 \\ +17 \\ \hline \end{array}$ 11. $\begin{array}{r} 13 \\ +5 \\ \hline \end{array}$

Subtract.

12. $74 - 8 =$ _____   13. $51 - 12 =$ _____   14. $60 - 15 =$ _____

15. $\begin{array}{r} 42 \\ -34 \\ \hline \end{array}$ 16. $\begin{array}{r} 78 \\ -29 \\ \hline \end{array}$ 17. $\begin{array}{r} 43 \\ -28 \\ \hline \end{array}$ 18. $\begin{array}{r} 50 \\ -18 \\ \hline \end{array}$

19. $\begin{array}{r} 80 \\ -37 \\ \hline \end{array}$ 20. $\begin{array}{r} 64 \\ -45 \\ \hline \end{array}$ 21. $\begin{array}{r} 28 \\ -14 \\ \hline \end{array}$ 22. $\begin{array}{r} 56 \\ -27 \\ \hline \end{array}$

Introduce Bar Graphs

VOCABULARY
horizontal bar graph
vertical bar graph

▶ Read a **Horizontal Bar Graph**

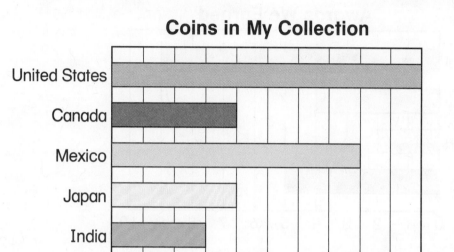

Coins in My Collection

▶ Read a **Vertical Bar Graph**

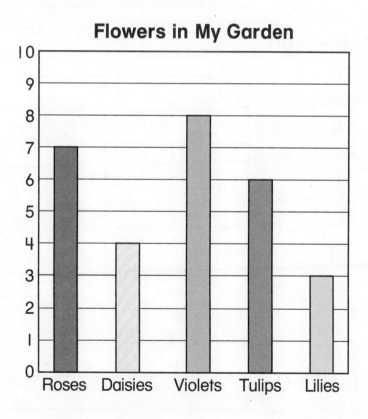

Flowers in My Garden

▶ Write Comparison Statements

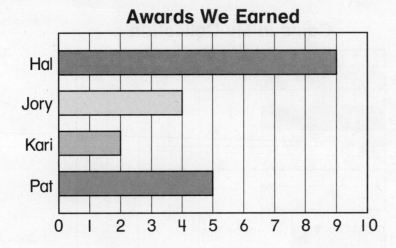

Awards We Earned

1. Use the horizontal bar graph.
   Write an *is greater than* statement.

   _____

   _____

▶ Make a Vertical Bar Graph

2. Make a vertical bar graph
   from the horizontal
   bar graph above.

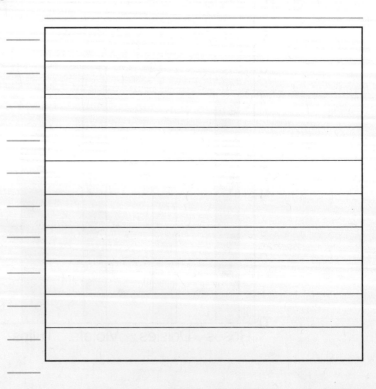

▶ Solve *Put Together/Take Apart* and *Compare* Problems

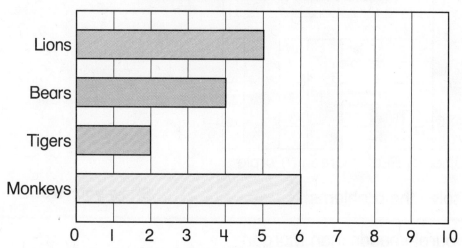

Animals at the Wildlife Park

Use the bar graph to solve the problems.   Show your work.

1. Four of the monkeys are adults and the rest are babies. How many of the monkeys are babies?

   ☐ _____
        label

2. How many fewer bears are there than monkeys?

   ☐ _____
        label

3. There are 2 fewer lions than elephants. How many elephants are there?

   ☐ _____
        label

▶ Solve Word Problems with More Than One Step

Jenny's Bead Collection

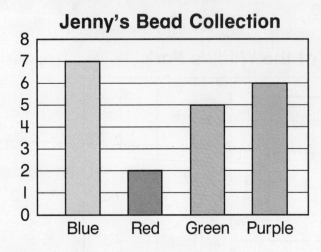

Use the bar graph to solve the problems.

© Houghton Mifflin Harcourt Publishing Company

Show your work.

4. Jenny has 4 fewer purple beads than Morgan.
   How many purple beads do Jenny and Morgan
   have in all?

   ☐ _____
   label

5. Morgan has 11 red beads. Then she gives 2 red
   beads to Arun. How many more red beads does
   Morgan have now than Jenny?

   ☐ _____
   label

6. Five of Jenny's beads are large and the rest
   are small. She buys some small yellow beads.
   Now she has 18 small beads. How many small
   yellow beads does she buy?

   ☐ _____
   label

Solve Problems Using a Bar Graph

► **What's the Error?**

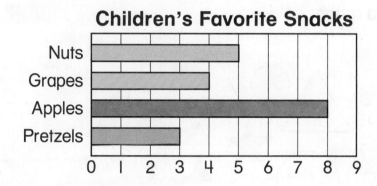

Children's Favorite Snacks

How many more children
choose fruit than nuts?

Fruit | 8
Nuts | 5 | ?

$$8 - 5 = 3$$

3 more children

Am I correct?

7. Show Puzzled Penguin how you
would solve the problem.

_____ more children

Name _____

▶ Organize and Graph Information

Here are some shapes for you to graph.

8. First make a **table**.

9. Then make a bar graph.

_____

	Number

Solve Problems Using a Bar Graph

VOCABULARY
survey
data

▶ Record the Collected Data

1. Show the results of your **survey** in the table.
   Your teacher will help you.

_____

_____	Number of Children

2. Show the **data** on a picture graph.

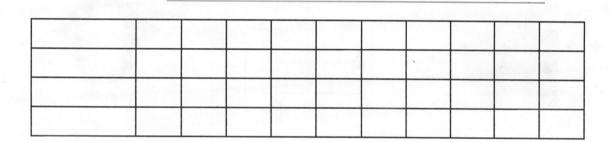

3. Show the data on a bar graph.

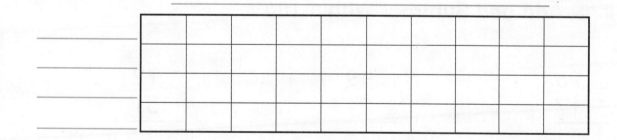

4. Use the data to write a 2-step word problem.

_____

_____

▶ What's the Error?

Favorite Subject	Number of Children
Reading	6
Math	7
Science	4
Art	4

Puzzled Penguin made a graph from the table.

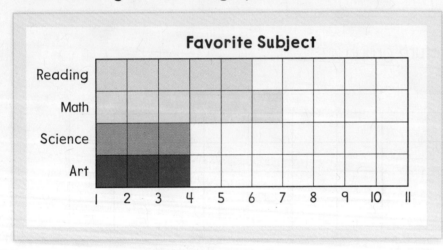

5. Fix Puzzled Penguin's errors.

▶ PATH to FLUENCY Add and Subtract Within 100

Add.

6. $\begin{array}{r} 76 \\ + 17 \\ \hline \end{array}$
    7. $\begin{array}{r} 49 \\ + 21 \\ \hline \end{array}$
    8. $\begin{array}{r} 12 \\ + 51 \\ \hline \end{array}$

Subtract.

9. $\begin{array}{r} 86 \\ - 28 \\ \hline \end{array}$
    10. $\begin{array}{r} 60 \\ - 37 \\ \hline \end{array}$
    11. $\begin{array}{r} 46 \\ - 19 \\ \hline \end{array}$

Collect and Graph Data

▶ Make Graphs Using Data from a Table

The table shows the number of bicycles sold at a store on four days last week.

Bicycle Sales

Day	Number Sold
Saturday	8
Sunday	9
Monday	3
Tuesday	4

1. Make a picture graph using data from the table.

2. Make a bar graph using data from the table.

▶ Solve Problems Using a Bar Graph

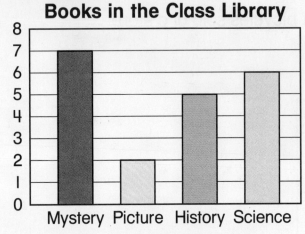

Books in the Class Library

Mystery Picture History Science

Use the bar graph to solve the problems.

Show your work.

3. Children are reading 3 history books.
   The rest are on the shelf in the library.
   How many history books are on the shelf?

   ☐ _____
   label

4. The class library has 2 more science books than
   math books. How many more math books must
   the library get so there is the same number of
   math books as mystery books?

   ☐ _____
   label

5. Children are reading some of the mystery books.
   The rest are on the shelf. The library gets 6 new
   mystery books. Now there are 10 mystery books on the
   shelf. How many mystery books are children reading?

   ☐ _____
   label

Make Graphs and Interpret Data

▶ Solve Problems Using a Bar Graph (continued)

Animals at a Farm

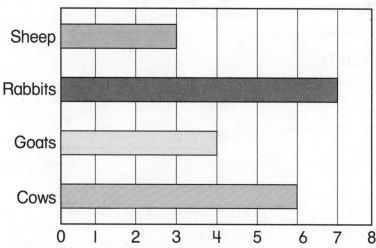

Use the bar graph to solve the problems.

Show your work.

---

6. The farm has 4 more rabbits than horses. How many horses does the farm have?

▢ _____
     label

---

7. The farm has 5 fewer goats than chickens. How many chickens does the farm have?

▢ _____
     label

---

8. There are 3 cows in the barn. The rest of the cows are in the field with the goats and the sheep. How many animals are in the field?

▢ _____
     label

▶ Solve *Compare* Problems with 2-Digit Numbers

Solve. Draw comparison bars for each.

9. A park has 46 maple trees. It has 18 fewer elm trees. How many elm trees are in the park?

   ☐ _____
   label

10. There are 62 pine trees in the park. There are 13 fewer pine trees than birch trees. How many birch trees are in the park?

    ☐ _____
    label

11. The park has 27 fir trees. There are 16 more spruce trees than fir trees. The park has 28 fewer spruce trees than oak trees. How many oak trees are in the park?

    ☐ _____
    label

► Math and Pets

Mrs. Pratt asks the children in her class to tell which kitten they think is the cutest of these four kittens.

Fluffy   Mink   Odin   Simba

The results of the survey are shown in this table.

Which Kitten Do You Think Is the Cutest?

Fluffy	○ ○ ○ ○ ○ ○
Mink	○ ○ ○ ○
Odin	○ ○ ○ ○ ○ ○ ○ ○ ○
Simba	○ ○ ○ ○ ○ ○

1. Use the information in the table to make a bar graph.

▶Take a Survey

Your teacher will ask all of the children in the class to tell which puppy they think is the cutest of these four puppies.

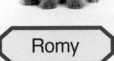
Romy Parker Domino Bernie

Show the results of the survey in this table.

Which Puppy Do You Think Is the Cutest?

Romy	
Parker	
Domino	
Bernie	

2. Use the information in the table to make a bar graph on your MathBoard.

3. Write a 2-step word problem that can be solved by using the graph. Trade problems with a classmate. Solve each other's problems.

Roses Picked

Roses Picked	
Brad	7
Mark	9
Pam	8
Luis	5

1. Make a picture graph to show the data
in the table.

Title: _____

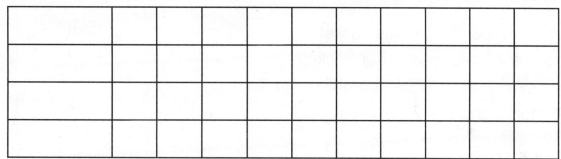

2. Make a bar graph to show the data
in the table.

Title: _____

Strawberries

Paula	🍓	🍓	🍓	🍓					
Reynaldo	🍓	🍓	🍓	🍓	🍓	🍓			

Use the picture graph. Write the number.
Ring more or fewer.

3. Paula has [   ] more fewer strawberries than Reynaldo.

_____

Solve these word problems.   **Show your work.**

4. Ray has 34 peaches in his basket.
   Maria has 19 peaches in her basket.
   How many more peaches does Ray
   have than Maria?

   [   ] _____
            label

_____

5. Michelle picks 28 apples. She
   picks 12 fewer than Hakim. How
   many apples does Hakim pick?

   [   ] _____
            label

_____

6. Kevin picks 12 more apples than Brendan.
   Kevin picks 50 apples. How many
   apples does Brendan pick?

   [   ] _____
            label

Use the bar graph. Write the number.
Ring more or fewer.

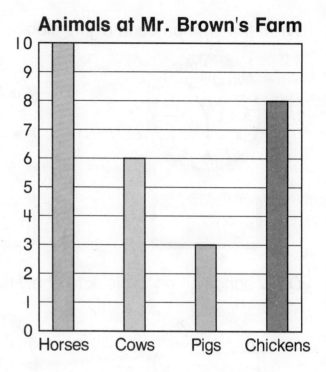

Animals at Mr. Brown's Farm

7. There are ☐ more fewer
   chickens than pigs.

8. There are ☐ animals at
   Mr. Brown's farm in all.

Use the bar graph to solve the problems.

9. Two of the cows are calves. The rest are adult
   cows. How many adult cows are there?

   ☐ _____

   label

10. There are 2 fewer chickens at Mrs. Smith's farm
    than at Mr. Brown's farm. How many chickens are
    there in all at the two farms?

    ☐ _____

    label

11. If Mr. Brown's farm gets 3 more horses, how many
    more horses than cows will there be?

    ☐ _____

    label

Write the time on each digital clock.

12.

13.

14.

Draw hands on each clock to show the time.

15.

8:10

16.

2:30

17.

12:00

For each activity, ring the time that makes sense.

18. wake up in the morning

7:00 P.M.   6:30 A.M.

19. go to the beach in the afternoon

9:00 A.M.   2:00 P.M.

20. **Extended Response** Explain how you can use skip counting to find the time shown on the clock.

_____

_____

_____

Dear Family:

In this unit, children will learn how to add 3-digit numbers that have totals up to 1,000.

Children begin the unit by learning to count to 1,000. They count by ones from a number, over the hundred, and into the next hundred. For example, 498, 499, 500, 501, 502, 503. You can help your child practice counting aloud to 1,000. Listen carefully as he or she crosses over the hundred.

Children will learn to write numbers to 1,000. Some children will write 5003 instead of 503 for five hundred three. Using Secret Code Cards will help children write the numbers correctly.

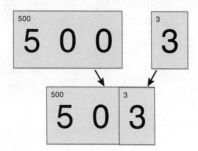

Help your child count small objects by making groups of 10 and then groups of 100. When the groups are made, help your child write the number of objects. This is a good way to help children recognize the difference between 5,003 and 503.

Please call if you have any questions or concerns. Thank you for helping your child learn about numbers to 1,000.

Sincerely,
Your child's teacher

Unit 6 includes the Common Core Standards for Mathematical Content for Operations and Algebraic Thinking 2.OA.1, Number and Operations in Base Ten 2.NBT.1, 2.NBT.1a, 2.NBT.1b, 2.NBT.2, 2.NBT.3, 2.NBT.4, 2.NBT.5, 2.NBT.7, 2.NBT.8, 2.NBT.9, Measurement and Data 2.MD.8, and all Mathematical Practices.

Estimada familia:

En esta unidad los niños aprenderán cómo sumar números de 3 dígitos con totales de hasta 1,000.

Los niños comienzan la unidad aprendiendo a contar hasta 1,000. Cuentan de uno en uno a partir de un número, llegan a la centena y comienzan con la siguiente centena. Por ejemplo, 498, 499, 500, 501, 502, 503. Puede ayudar a su niño a practicar, contando en voz alta hasta 1,000. Ponga atención cada vez que llegue a una nueva centena.

Los niños aprenderán a escribir los números hasta 1,000. Tal vez, algunos niños escriban 5003 en vez de 503 al intentar escribir quinientos tres. Usar las Tarjetas de código secreto los ayudará a escribir correctamente los números.

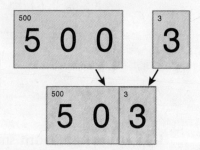

Ayude a su niño a contar objetos pequeños formando grupos de 10 y luego, grupos de 100. Cuando formen los grupos, ayúdelo a escribir el número de objetos. Esta es una buena manera de ayudar a los niños a reconocer la diferencia entre 5,003 y 503.

Si tiene alguna duda o pregunta, por favor comuníquese conmigo. Gracias por ayudar a su niño a aprender a contar hasta 1,000.

Atentamente,
El maestro de su niño

COMMON CORE

La Unidad 6 incluye los Common Core Standards for Mathematical Content for Operations and Algebraic Thinking 2.OA.1, Number and Operations in Base Ten 2.NBT.1, 2.NBT.1a, 2.NBT.1b, 2.NBT.2, 2.NBT.3, 2.NBT.4, 2.NBT.5, 2.NBT.7, 2.NBT.8, 2.NBT.9, Measurement and Data 2.MD.8, and all Mathematical Practices.

▶ Count to 1,000 by Hundreds

© Houghton Mifflin Harcourt Publishing Company

Cut on dashed lines.

Dollars with Penny Array (back)

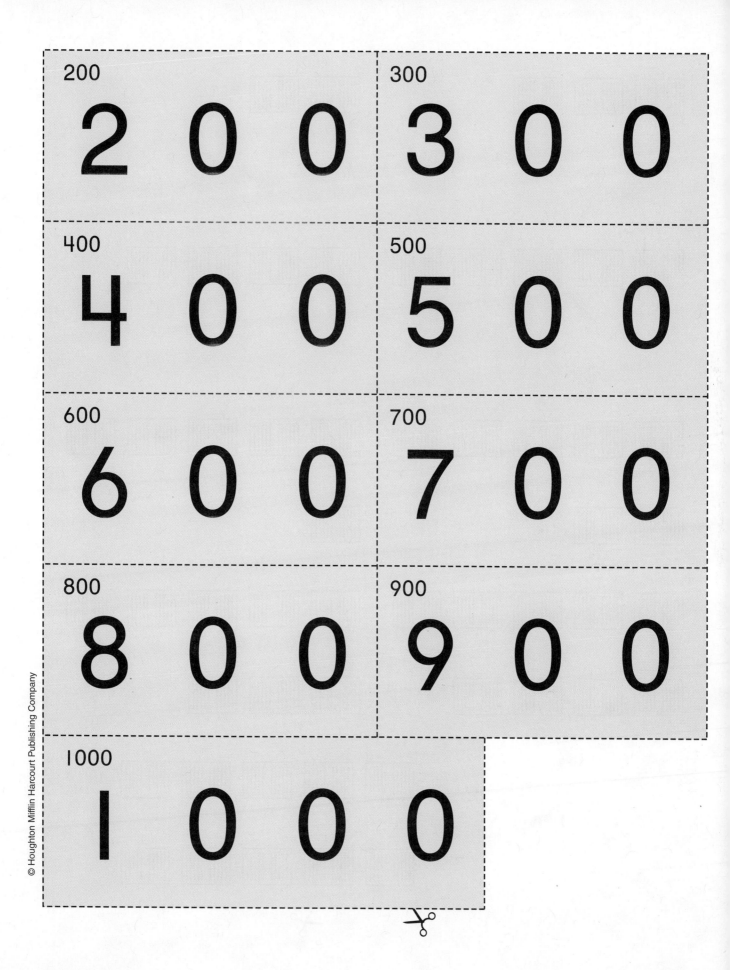

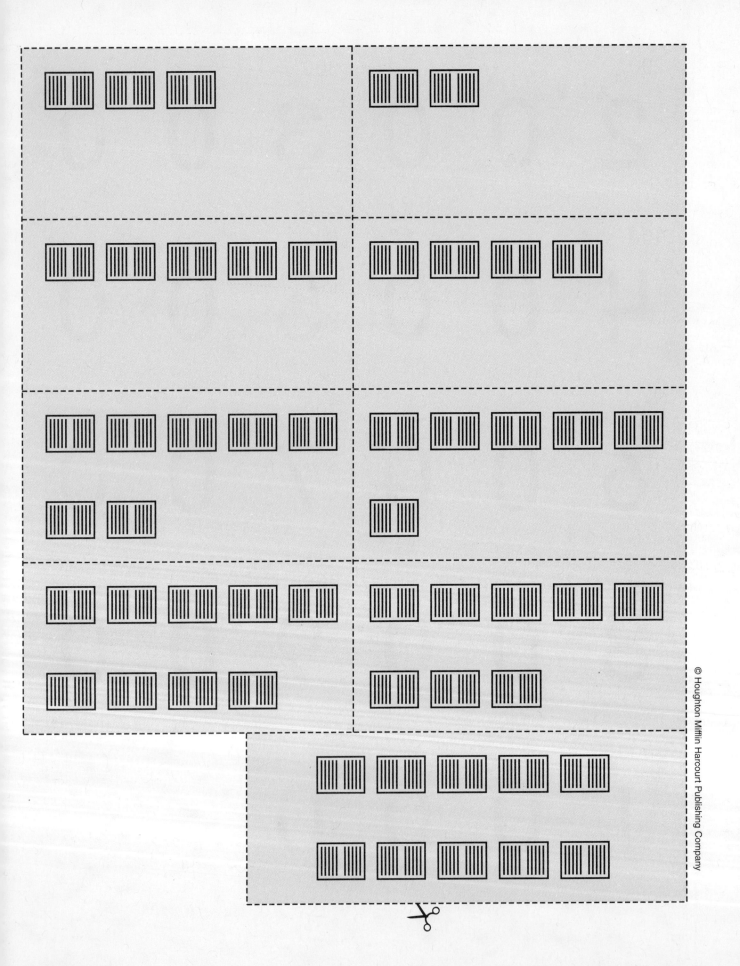

Secret Code Cards (200–1000)

▶ Review the Use of Boxes, Sticks, and Circles to Represent Numbers

Write the number that is shown by the drawing.

1. ☐ ☐ ☐ ☐ ☐   ☐ |||| ||

_____   _____   _____   Total _____

Hundreds   Tens   Ones

2. ☐ ☐ ☐ ||| ○○○○○

_____   _____   _____   Total _____

Hundreds   Tens   Ones

3. ☐ ☐ ☐   ○○○○○ ○○○○

_____   _____   _____   Total _____

Hundreds   Tens   Ones

Draw boxes, sticks, and circles to show the number.

4. 740

_____

5. 876

_____

6. 294

_____

7. 502

► **Expanded Form**

Write the hundreds, tens, and ones.

8. 382 = <u>300</u> + <u>80</u> + <u>2</u>
 H T O

9. 738 = ____ + ____ + ____

10. 526 = ____ + ____ + ____

11. 267 = ____ + ____ + ____

Write the number.

12. 400 + 50 + 9 = <u>459</u>
 H T O

13. 800 + 10 + 3 = ____

14. 100 + 70 + 5 = ____

15. 600 + 40 + 1 = ____

Write the number that makes the equation true.

16. ____ = 5 + 900 + 40

17. 7 + 200 = ____

18. ____ = 400 + 6 + 80

19. 800 + 40 = ____

20. ____ = 70 + 300

21. 60 + 500 + 3 = ____

22. ____ = 2 + 400

23. 9 + 90 + 200 = ____

24. 462 = 2 + 400 + ____

25. ____ + 90 + 700 = 798

26. 523 = 20 + 3 + ____

27. ____ + 4 + 200 = 224

Place Value

▶ **Solve and Discuss**

Write <, >, or =.

1. 635 ◯ 735   2. 527 ◯ 527

3. 820 ◯ 518   4. 327 ◯ 372

5. 975 ◯ 987   6. 321 ◯ 567

7. 267 ◯ 267   8. 271 ◯ 172

9. 654 ◯ 564   10. 750 ◯ 507

▶ **What's the Error?**

35 ⬤> 245

I know that 3 is greater than 2. Did I make a mistake?

11. Draw boxes, sticks, and circles to help Puzzled Penguin.

35 ◯ 245

► **Compare Numbers**

Write <, >, or =.

12. 620 ◯ 62	13. 510 ◯ 150
14. 852 ◯ 852	15. 854 ◯ 984
16. 71 ◯ 315	17. 357 ◯ 218
18. 418 ◯ 387	19. 482 ◯ 501
20. 359 ◯ 359	21. 376 ◯ 476
22. 291 ◯ 191	23. 333 ◯ 9

► **PATH to FLUENCY Add or Subtract Within 100**

Add.

24. 35 + 7 = _____   25. 6 + 77 = _____   26. 12 + 4 = _____

27. 19
    +60
    _____

28. 35
    +42
    _____

29. 27
    +73
    _____

30. 58
    + 4
    _____

Subtract.

31. 100
    − 52
    _____

32. 98
    − 35
    _____

33. 83
    −78
    _____

34. 71
    −35
    _____

Compare Numbers Within 999

► Count Over a Hundred by Ones and by Tens

Count by ones. Write the numbers.

1. 396　397　_398_　_399_　_400_　_401_　_402_　_403_　404

2. 594　595　____　____　____　____　____　____　602

3. 297　298　____　____　____　____　____　____　305

4. 495　____　____　____　____　____　____　____　503

5. 598　____　____　____　____　____　____　____　606

6. 697　____　____　____　____　____　____　____　705

Count by tens. Write the numbers.

7. 460　470　_480_　_490_　_500_　_510_　_520_　_530_　540

8. 370　380　____　____　____　____　____　____　450

9. 640　650　____　____　____　____　____　____　720

10. 580　____　____　____　____　____　____　____　660

11. 750　____　____　____　____　____　____　____　830

12. 830　____　____　____　____　____　____　____　910

Name _____

▶ Read and Write Number Names

You can write numbers with words or symbols.

1 one	11 eleven	10 ten	100 one hundred
2 two	12 twelve	20 twenty	200 two hundred
3 three	13 thirteen	30 thirty	300 three hundred
4 four	14 fourteen	40 forty	400 four hundred
5 five	15 fifteen	50 fifty	500 five hundred
6 six	16 sixteen	60 sixty	600 six hundred
7 seven	17 seventeen	70 seventy	700 seven hundred
8 eight	18 eighteen	80 eighty	800 eight hundred
9 nine	19 nineteen	90 ninety	900 nine hundred
			1,000 one thousand

Write each number.

13. one hundred twenty-five _____

14. four hundred fifty-eight _____

15. six hundred thirty-one _____

16. nine hundred sixty-two _____

17. eight hundred forty _____

18. seven hundred three _____

Write each number name.

19. 500 _____

20. 592 _____

21. 650 _____

22. 605 _____

23. 1,000 _____

Count by Ones and by Tens

▶ Add Numbers with 1, 2, and 3 Digits

Solve.

1. $200 + 200 =$ _____ $200 + 20 =$ _____ $200 + 2 =$ _____

   $300 + 300 =$ _____ $300 + 30 =$ _____ $300 + 3 =$ _____

   $400 + 400 =$ _____ $400 + 40 =$ _____ $400 + 4 =$ _____

   $500 + 500 =$ _____ $500 + 50 =$ _____ $500 + 5 =$ _____

2. $600 + 200 =$ _____ $20 + 600 =$ _____ $2 + 600 =$ _____

   $700 + 300 =$ _____ $30 + 700 =$ _____ $3 + 700 =$ _____

   $800 + 100 =$ _____ $10 + 800 =$ _____ $1 + 800 =$ _____

   $900 + 100 =$ _____ $10 + 900 =$ _____ $1 + 900 =$ _____

   $100 + 900 =$ _____ $90 + 100 =$ _____ $9 + 100 =$ _____

3. $100 + 134 =$ _____ $100 + 34 =$ _____ $4 + 100 =$ _____

   $200 + 245 =$ _____ $200 + 45 =$ _____ $200 + 5 =$ _____

   $300 + 356 =$ _____ $56 + 300 =$ _____ $6 + 300 =$ _____

   $400 + 467 =$ _____ $400 + 67 =$ _____ $400 + 7 =$ _____

   $500 + 478 =$ _____ $78 + 500 =$ _____ $8 + 500 =$ _____

▶ Solve and Discuss

Solve each word problem. Use Secret Code Cards
or draw proof drawings if you wish.

4. A camping club buys some
   raisins. They buy 3 cartons
   that have 100 bags each. They
   also have 24 bags left from their
   last trip. How many bags of
   raisins does the club have?

   ☐ _____
   label

5. Two friends want to make
   necklaces. They buy 1 package
   of one hundred red beads,
   1 package of one hundred blue
   beads, and 1 package of one
   hundred green beads. They
   already have 12 loose beads.
   How many beads do they have
   altogether?

   ☐ _____
   label

6. Mia and Bo want to advertise
   their yard sale. They decide
   to make fliers. They buy
   2 packs of paper. Each pack
   has 200 sheets in it. They have
   32 sheets in their art box.
   How many sheets of paper
   do they have?

   ☐ _____
   label

7. All of the students at a school
   go out on the playground. They
   form 8 groups of one hundred
   students and 6 groups of ten.
   There are 5 students left.
   How many students go to this
   school?

   ☐ _____
   label

Family Letter

Dear Family:

Your child is now learning how to add 3-digit numbers. The methods children use are similar to those used for adding 2-digit numbers.

New Groups Below

Step 1	Step 2	Step 3
456	456	456
+278	+278	+278
4	34	734

100   10

400

200

Children put the new 1 hundred or 1 ten on the line instead of at the top of the column. Many children find this less confusing because:

• They can see the 14.

• It is easier to add the 1 after they add the 5 and the 7.

Show All Totals

456
+278
hundreds → 600
tens → 120
ones → 14
734

Children see the hundreds, tens, and ones they are adding. These also can be seen when they make a math drawing like the one above.

Children may use any method that they understand, can explain, and can do fairly quickly. They should use hundreds, tens, and ones language to explain. This shows that they understand that they are adding 4 hundreds and 2 hundreds and not 4 and 2.

Please call if you have questions or comments.

Sincerely,
Your child's teacher

© Houghton Mifflin Harcourt Publishing Company

COMMON CORE
Unit 6 includes the Common Core Standards for Mathematical Content for Operations and Algebraic Thinking 2.OA.1, Number and Operations in Base Ten 2.NBT.1, 2.NBT.1a, 2.NBT.1b, 2.NBT.2, 2.NBT.3, 2.NBT.4, 2.NBT.5, 2.NBT.7, 2.NBT.8, 2.NBT.9, Measurement and Data 2.MD.8, and all Mathematical Practices.

Carta a la familia

Estimada familia:

Ahora su niño está aprendiendo a sumar números de 3 dígitos. Los métodos que los niños usarán son semejantes a los usados para sumar numeros de 2 dígitos.

Grupos nuevos abajo

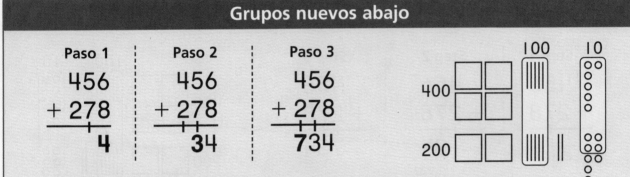

Paso 1	Paso 2	Paso 3
456	456	456
+ 278	+ 278	+ 278
4	34	734

Los niños ponen la nueva centena o decena en la línea en vez de ponerla arriba de la columna. A muchos niños esto les resulta menos confuso porque:

- Pueden ver el 14.
- Es más fácil sumar el 1 después de que sumaron 5 y 7.

Mostrar todos los totales

456
+ 278

centenas → 600
decenas → 120
unidades → 14
734

Los niños ven las centenas, las decenas y las unidades que están sumando. Esto también se puede observar cuando hacen un dibujo matemático como el de arriba.

Los niños pueden usar cualquier método que comprendan, puedan explicar y puedan hacer relativamente rápido. Para explicar deben usar un lenguaje relacionado con centenas, decenas y unidades. Esto demuestra que entienden que están sumando 4 centenas y 2 centenas, y no 4 y 2.

Si tiene alguna duda o pregunta, por favor comuníquese conmigo.

Atentamente,
El maestro de su niño

COMMON CORE La Unidad 6 incluye los Common Core Standards for Mathematical Content for Operations and Algebraic Thinking 2.OA.1, Number and Operations in Base Ten 2.NBT.1, 2.NBT.1a, 2.NBT.1b, 2.NBT.2, 2.NBT.3, 2.NBT.4, 2.NBT.5, 2.NBT.7, 2.NBT.8, 2.NBT.9, Measurement and Data 2.MD.8, and all Mathematical Practices.

3-Digit Addition

▶ Solve and Discuss

Solve each word problem.
Be ready to explain what you did.

1. Milo makes a display of plant and fish fossils for the library. He puts in 478 plant fossils. He puts in 67 fish fossils. How many fossils are in the display?

   [   ] _____
          label

2. The nature club plants some pine and birch trees. They plant 496 birch trees. Then they plant 283 pine trees. How many trees does the club plant in all?

   [   ] _____
          label

3. There are 818 ducks entered in the Rubber Duck River Race. Then 182 more are added. How many ducks are in the race now?

   [   ] _____
          label

4. There are 189 children at Camp Sunshine. There are 375 children at Camp Bluebird. How many children are there at the two camps?

   [   ] _____
          label

▶ Practice 3-Digit Addition

Add using any method. Make a proof drawing if it helps.

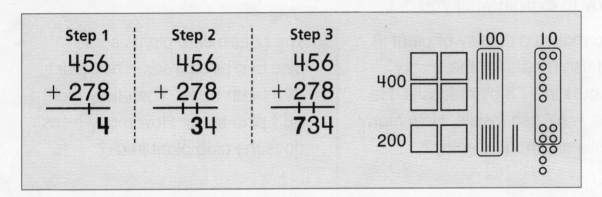

Step 1	Step 2	Step 3
456	456	456
+ 278	+ 278	+ 278
4	34	734

5. 375
   +482

6. 148
   +236

7. 584
   + 61

8. 168
   +674

9.   89
   +376

10. 563
    +157

11. 497
    +259

12. 124
    +563

13. 348
    +239

▶ New Ten or New Hundred

Add. Use any method. Make a proof drawing if it helps.

1.
$$236 \\ +478$$

Make a new ten? _____

Make a new hundred? _____

2. $183 + 517 =$ _____

Make a new ten? _____

Make a new hundred? _____

3. $93 + 485 =$ _____

Make a new ten? _____

Make a new hundred? _____

4.
$$368 \\ +257$$

Make a new ten? _____

Make a new hundred? _____

5. $347 + 37 =$ _____

Make a new ten? _____

Make a new hundred? _____

6. $645 + 87 =$ _____

Make a new ten? _____

Make a new hundred? _____

► New Ten, New Hundred, or New Thousand

Add. Use any method. Draw a proof drawing if it helps.

7.　195
　　+172

Make a new ten? _____

Make a new hundred? _____

Make a new thousand? _____

8.　300
　　+700

Make a new ten? _____

Make a new hundred? _____

Make a new thousand? _____

9. 360 + 640 = _____

Make a new ten? _____

Make a new hundred? _____

Make a new thousand? _____

10. 75 + 823 = _____

Make a new ten? _____

Make a new hundred? _____

Make a new thousand? _____

11. 905 + 95 = _____

Make a new ten? _____

Make a new hundred? _____

Make a new thousand? _____

12. 413 + 587 = _____

Make a new ten? _____

Make a new hundred? _____

Make a new thousand? _____

▶ Find the Hidden Animal

Directions for the puzzle on page 276.

1. Start by coloring in the six dotted squares. These are "free" squares. They are part of the puzzle solution.

2. Find one of the sums below. Then look for that sum in the puzzle grid. Color in that puzzle piece.

3. Find all 20 sums. Color the puzzle pieces with the sums. Color in all 20 correct answers.

4. Name the hidden animal. It is a(n) _____.

524 +247	287 +164	384 +375	456 +174	327 +265
207 +595	248 +376	282 +457	548 +387	233 +288
367 +265	293 +595	284 +376	537 +463	138 +327
286 + 78	407 +266	503 +148	78 +65	192 +339

See page 275 for directions on how to solve the puzzle.

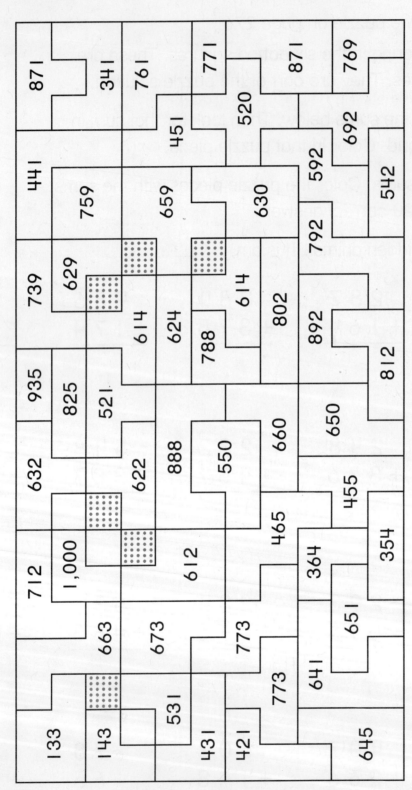

Discuss 3-Digit Addition

▶ Adding Up to Solve Word Problems

Solve each word problem.

Show your work.

---

1. Mr. Cruz has 750 yams to sell. He sells some and has 278 yams left. How many yams does he sell?

   ☐ _____
          label

---

2. At the end of February there are 692 houses in our town. Some new houses are built in March. At the end of March there are 976 houses. How many houses are built in March?

   ☐ _____
          label

---

3. Delia has 524 rocks in her collection. She gives some to her sister. Now she has 462 rocks. How many rocks did she give away?

   ☐ _____
          label

---

4. On Saturday, 703 people go to a movie. 194 go in the afternoon. The rest go in the evening. How many people go in the evening?

   ☐ _____
          label

▶ Adding Up to Solve Word Problems (continued)

Solve each word problem.   Show your work.

5. Jeremy makes 525 coasters that are circles or squares as gifts for his family. 347 coasters are circles. How many coasters are squares?

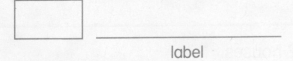

               label

6. Analisse has 419 marbles. 287 of the marbles are blue. How many marbles are other colors?

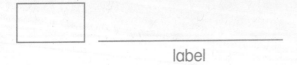

               label

▶ PATH to FLUENCY Add and Subtract Within 100

Add.

7.	8.	9.	10.
32	42	57	44
+ 50	+ 57	+ 43	+ 7

Subtract.

11.	12.	13.	14.
98	100	43	61
− 24	− 31	− 38	− 29

Family Letter

Dear Family:

Your child is now learning how to subtract 3-digit numbers. The most important part is understanding and being able to explain a method. Children may use any method that they understand, can explain, and can perform fairly quickly.

Expanded Method

Step 1   Step 2

$$432 = 400 + 30 + 2 = \overset{\overset{\textstyle 120}{300 \;\; \cancel{20}}}{\cancel{400} + \cancel{30} + 2} \;\; 12$$
$$-\,273 = 200 + 70 + 3 = 200 + 70 + 3$$

Step 3 $\begin{cases} 100 + 50 + 9 \\ = 159 \end{cases}$

Step 1 "Expand" each number to show that it is made up of hundreds, tens, and ones.

Step 2 Check to see if there are enough ones to subtract from. If not, ungroup a ten into 10 ones and add it to the existing ones. Check to see if there are enough tens to subtract from. If not, ungroup a hundred into 10 tens and add it to the existing tens. Children may also ungroup from the left.

Step 3 Subtract to find the answer. Children may subtract from left to right or right to left.

Ungroup First Method

Step 1 Check to see if there are enough ones and tens to subtract from. Ungroup where needed.

Look inside 432. Ungroup 432 and rename it as 3 hundreds, 12 tens, and 12 ones.

Ungroup from the left:

Ungroup from the right:

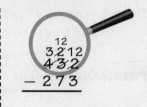

Step 2 Subtract to find the answer. Children may subtract from the left or from the right.

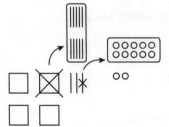

In explaining any method they use, children are expected to use "hundreds, tens, and ones" language and drawings to show that they understand place value.

Please call if you have questions or comments.

Sincerely,
Your child's teacher

COMMON CORE — Unit 6 includes the Common Core Standards for Mathematical Content for Operations and Algebraic Thinking 2.OA.1, Number and Operations in Base Ten 2.NBT.1, 2.NBT.1a, 2.NBT.1b, 2.NBT.2, 2.NBT.3, 2.NBT.4, 2.NBT.7, 2.NBT.8, 2.NBT.9, Measurement and Data 2.MD.8, and all Mathematical Practices.

Estimada familia:

Su niño está aprendiendo a restar números de 3 dígitos. Lo más importante es comprender y saber explicar un método. Los niños pueden usar cualquier método que comprendan, puedan explicar y puedan hacer relativamente rápido.

Método extendido

Paso 1   **Paso 2**

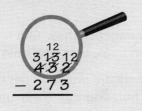

$$432 = 400 + 30 + 2 = 400 + 30 + 2$$
$$- 273 = 200 + 70 + 3 = 200 + 70 + 3$$

Paso 3 $\begin{cases} 100 + 50 + 9 \\ = 159 \end{cases}$

Paso 1 "Extender" cada número para mostrar que consta de centenas, decenas y unidades.

Paso 2 Observar si hay suficientes unidades para restar. Si no, desagrupar una decena para formar 10 unidades y sumarlas a las unidades existentes. Observar si hay suficientes decenas para restar. Si no, desagrupar una centena para formar 10 decenas y sumarlas a las decenas existentes. Los niños también pueden desagrupar por la izquierda.

Paso 3 Restar para hallar la respuesta. Los niños pueden restar de izquierda a derecha o de derecha a izquierda.

Método de desagrupar primero

Paso 1 Observar si hay suficientes unidades y decenas para restar. Desagrupar cuando haga falta.

Mirar dentro de 432. Desagrupar 432 y volver a nombrarlo como 3 centenas, 12 decenas y 12 unidades.

Desagrupar por la izquierda: **Desagrupar por la derecha:**

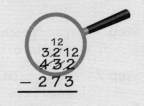

Paso 2 Restar para hallar la respuesta. Los niños pueden restar empezando por la izquierda o por la derecha.

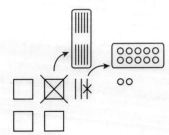

Para explicar cualquier método que usen, los niños deben usar lenguaje y dibujos relacionados con centenas, decenas y unidades para demostrar que comprenden el valor posicional.

Si tiene alguna duda o comentario, por favor comuníquese conmigo.

Atentamente,
El maestro de su niño

COMMON CORE

La Unidad 6 incluye los Common Core Standards for Mathematical Content for Operations and Algebraic Thinking 2.OA.1, Number and Operations in Base Ten 2.NBT.1, 2.NBT.1a, 2.NBT.1b, 2.NBT.2, 2.NBT.3, 2.NBT.4, 2.NBT.7, 2.NBT.8, 2.NBT.9, Measurement and Data 2.MD.8, and all Mathematical Practices.

Subtract from Hundreds Numbers

► **Discuss Subtraction Problems**

Solve each word problem. Use any method.
Make a proof drawing.

1. A teacher buys 200 erasers for his students. He gives 152 of them away. How many erasers does he have left over?

   □ _____
   label

2. The school cafeteria has 500 apples. Some of them are served with lunch. After lunch, there are 239 apples left. How many apples does the cafeteria serve?

   □ _____
   label

3. Teresa sells guitars. She has 600 guitars. She sells 359. How many guitars does she have left?

   □ _____
   label

4. Jorge is on a basketball team. He scores 181 points one year. He scores some points in a second year, too. He scores a total of 400 points over the two years. How many points does he score the second year?

   □ _____
   label

► Practice Subtracting from 1,000

Subtract. Use any method.

5.
```
  1,0 0 0
 −  7 7 2
```

6.
```
  1,0 0 0
 −  5 2 6
```

7.
```
  1,0 0 0
 −  8 4 3
```

8.
```
  1,0 0 0
 −  2 9 3
```

9.
```
  1,0 0 0
 −    9 5
```

10.
```
  1,0 0 0
 −  1 5 7
```

11. Elliot has 1,000 pennies. He puts 350 pennies in penny rolls. How many pennies are left?

12. Marta's class plans to collect 1,000 cans this year. They have 452 cans so far. How many more cans do they plan to collect?

[_____]
_____
label

[_____]
_____
label

VOCABULARY
ungroup

▶ Do I Need to Ungroup?

Decide if you need to **ungroup**. If you need to ungroup, draw a magnifying glass around the top number. Then find the answer.

1.
$$
\begin{array}{r}
5\ 0\ 8 \\
-\ 3\ 4\ 6 \\
\hline
\end{array}
$$

Ungroup to get 10 ones? _____

Ungroup to get 10 tens? _____

2.
$$
\begin{array}{r}
5\ 0\ 0 \\
-\ 3\ 0\ 6 \\
\hline
\end{array}
$$

Ungroup to get 10 ones? _____

Ungroup to get 10 tens? _____

3.
$$
\begin{array}{r}
6\ 7\ 0 \\
-\ 3\ 4\ 0 \\
\hline
\end{array}
$$

Ungroup to get 10 ones? _____

Ungroup to get 10 tens? _____

4.
$$
\begin{array}{r}
5\ 7\ 0 \\
-\ 3\ 9\ 0 \\
\hline
\end{array}
$$

Ungroup to get 10 ones? _____

Ungroup to get 10 tens? _____

Name _____

▶ Subtract from 3-Digit Numbers with Zeros

Subtract.

5.
```
   406
 - 181
```

6.
```
   790
 - 272
```

7.
```
   340
 - 118
```

8.
```
   507
 - 438
```

9.
```
   400
 - 263
```

10.
```
   500
 - 234
```

▶ (PATH to FLUENCY) Add and Subtract Within 100

Add.

11.
```
   38
 + 44
```

12.
```
   61
 + 17
```

13.
```
   36
 + 64
```

14.
```
   78
 + 19
```

Subtract.

15.
```
   100
 -  57
```

16.
```
   92
 - 40
```

17.
```
   64
 - 25
```

18.
```
   81
 - 19
```

▶Review Addition and Subtraction

Ring *add* or *subtract*. Check if you need to ungroup or make a new ten or hundred. Then find the answer.

1.
```
   762
 - 395
```

Subtract

☐ Ungroup to get 10 ones

☐ Ungroup to get 10 tens

Add

☐ Make 1 new ten

☐ Make 1 new hundred

2.
```
   395
 + 367
```

Subtract

☐ Ungroup to get 10 ones

☐ Ungroup to get 10 tens

Add

☐ Make 1 new ten

☐ Make 1 new hundred

3.
```
   287
 - 193
```

Subtract

☐ Ungroup to get 10 ones

☐ Ungroup to get 10 tens

Add

☐ Make 1 new ten

☐ Make 1 new hundred

4.
```
   437
 + 324
```

Subtract

☐ Ungroup to get 10 ones

☐ Ungroup to get 10 tens

Add

☐ Make 1 new ten

☐ Make 1 new hundred

VOCABULARY
opposite operation

► Relate Addition and Subtraction

Decide whether you need to add or subtract.

Draw a Math Mountain. Check your answer by using

the **opposite operation**.

5. 532
   − 1 8 1   ✓

6. 532
   + 1 8 1   ✓

7. 528
   + 3 5 7   ✓

8. 1,000
   − 4 3 8   ✓

9. 571
   + 2 8 7   ✓

10. 904
    − 4 5 8   ✓

Relationships Between Addition and Subtraction Methods

▶Solve and Discuss

Make a drawing. Write an equation.
Solve the problem.

1. Lucero spills a bag of marbles. 219 fall on the floor. 316 are still in the bag. How many were in the bag in the beginning?

[   ] _____
        label

2. Al counts bugs in the park. He counts 561 on Monday. He counts 273 fewer than that on Tuesday. How many bugs does he count on Tuesday?

[   ] _____
        label

3. Happy the Clown gives out balloons. She gives out 285 at the zoo and then she gives out some more at the amusement park. Altogether she gives out 503. How many balloons does she give out at the amusement park?

[   ] _____
        label

4. Charlie the Clown gives out 842 balloons at the fun fair. He gives out 194 at the store. He gives out 367 at the playground. How many more balloons does he give out at the fun fair than at the playground?

[   ] _____
        label

▶ Solve and Discuss (continued)

Make a drawing. Write an equation. Solve the problem.

5. Damon collects stamps. He has 383 stamps. Then he buys 126 more at a yard sale. How many stamps does he have now?

☐ _____
   label

6. Mr. Lewis sells 438 melons. Now he has 294 melons left. How many melons did he have at the start?

☐ _____
   label

7. Ali is giving out ribbons for a race. She gave out 57 ribbons so far, and she has 349 ribbons left. How many ribbons did she have at the start?

☐ _____
   label

8. Cora collected 542 sports cards last year. She collected 247 fewer than that this year. How many cards did she collect in both years together?

☐ _____
   label

Mixed Addition and Subtraction Word Problems

▶ Solve and Discuss (continued)

Make a drawing. Write an equation. Solve the problem.

9. Tanya is working on a puzzle. She has placed 643 pieces. There are 1,000 pieces in the puzzle. How many more pieces does she have to place?

 _____
label

10. In March the Shaws plant some flowers. In April they plant 178 more flowers. In the two months they plant a total of 510 flowers. How many flowers do they plant in March?

 _____
label

11. Jeremy has 48 action figures. Jeremy has 14 more action figures than Keith. How many action figures does Keith have?

 _____
label

12. Pawel gives out fliers about a play. He gives out 194 fliers at the bakery. He gives out 358 at the grocery store. How many fewer fliers does he give out at the bakery than at the grocery store?

 _____
label

► **Solve and Discuss** (continued)

Make a drawing. Write an equation. Solve the problem.

13. Rue has 842 buttons. Then she gives some to a friend. Now she has 263 buttons. How many buttons does Rue give to her friend?

_____
label

14. Last week Jan sold some tickets to a play. She sells 345 more this week. Altogether she sells 500 tickets. How many tickets did she sell last week?

_____
label

15. April has 98 fewer pennies than Julie has. April has 521 pennies. How many pennies does Julie have?

_____
label

16. There are 675 plastic cups and 300 paper plates in a cabinet. Jaime puts more cups and plates in the cabinet. Now there are 850 cups. How many cups does Jaime add?

_____
label

Mixed Addition and Subtraction Word Problems

▶ **Math and Artists**

Many artists sell their
work at art fairs.

Solve.

---

1. On one weekend, 489 people come to the art fair on
   Saturday and 511 people come to the fair on Sunday.
   How many people come to the fair in all?

   ☐ _____
   label

---

2. Wendy uses silver and blue beads to make
   necklaces to sell. She uses 72 blue beads.
   She uses 38 more blue beads than silver beads.
   How many silver beads does she use?

   ☐ _____
   label

---

3. LeBron uses tiny seed beads to make bracelets.
   He buys a package of seed beads with 350 red
   beads and 250 white beads. After he makes
   the bracelets for the fair, he has just 6 beads left.
   How many beads does he use?

   ☐ _____
   label

► Caricatures

A caricature is a drawing of a person.
The drawing looks like a cartoon.

- Last week, an artist drew
  146 children and 84 adults.

- This week, the artist drew
  167 children and 55 adults.

Solve. Use the information in the box above.

4. How many people did the artist draw last week?

> label

5. How many people did the artist draw this week?

> label

6. How many fewer people did the artist draw
this week than last week?

> label

7. Did the artist draw more children or more adults?

more

Focus on Mathematical Practices

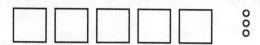
1. Write the number that is shown by the drawing.

☐ ☐ ☐ ☐ ☐   ⦂·

_____   _____   _____   Total _____
Hundreds   Tens   Ones

Write the hundreds, tens, and ones.
Then write the number name.
Example: 456 = __400__ + __50__ + __6__   __four hundred fifty-six__

2. 915 = ____ + ____ + ____   _____

3. 263 = ____ + ____ + ____   _____

4. Count by 1s. Write the numbers.

294 295 ____ ____ ____ ____ ____ 302

5. Count by 10s. Write the numbers.

340 350 ____ ____ ____ ____ ____ 420

6. Count by 100s. Write the numbers.

200 300 ____ ____ ____ ____ ____ 1,000

Write <, >, or =.

7. 265 256   8. 95 509   9. 815 ◯ 815

Add.

10.
```
   7 4 5
 + 1 3 8
```

11.
```
   3 7 7
 + 6 2 3
```

12. 394 + 10 = _____

13. 198 + 56 = _____

Subtract.

14. 596 − 100 = _____

15. 603 − 10 = _____

16.
```
   7 8 2
 − 5 2 8
```

17.
```
   4 4 7
 − 1 7 8
```

Subtract.

18.
```
  5 0 5
- 3 7 1
```

19.
```
  3 0 0
- 2 3 9
```

20. $618 - 73 =$ _____

21. $1{,}000 - 272 =$ _____

Solve.   Show your work.

22. Mia has 45 cards in her collection. This is 39 fewer
cards than her friend Letty has. How many cards
does Letty have in her collection?

_____
label

23. This morning 256 books were returned to
the library. 596 more were returned
this afternoon. How many books were
returned altogether?

_____
label

Solve.   **Show your work.**

24. Ada read 124 pages in a book.
    The book has 300 pages. How many
    more pages does she still have to
    read to finish the book?

    ┌─────────┐
    │   │ _____
    └─────────┘   label

25. **Extended Response** Show and explain how to
    subtract 279 from 458. Use the words *hundreds*,
    tens, and *ones*. Explain how and why you can use
    addition to check your answer.

Family Letter

Dear Family:

In this unit, your child will learn about rectangular arrays and how to use addition to count the number of objects in an array. The array below has 2 rows and 3 columns. It can be described as 2 rows with 3 tiles in each row or 3 columns with 2 tiles in each column.

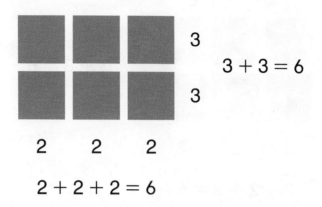

$$3 + 3 = 6$$

$$2 + 2 + 2 = 6$$

You can help your child by working with him or her to practice using the words *array*, *rows*, and *columns*. For example, ask your child to use pennies or other small objects to make an array that has 4 rows with 5 objects in each row. Ask your child to write the addition equations that show the total number of objects in the array. ($5 + 5 + 5 + 5 = 20$ and $4 + 4 + 4 + 4 + 4 = 20$)

Your child will also be learning about equal parts of circles and rectangles: 2 *halves*, 3 *thirds*, and 4 *fourths*. You can practice using this vocabulary at home. For example, "I am cutting this pizza into 4 fourths."

Please call if you have any questions or concerns.

Sincerely,
Your child's teacher

COMMON CORE

Unit 7 includes the Common Core Standards for Mathematical Content for Operations and Algebraic Thinking 2.OA.1, 2.OA.3, 2.OA.4, Geometry 2.G.1, 2.G.2, 2.G.3, Measurement and Data 2.MD.5, 2.MD.6, and all Mathematical Practices.

Estimada familia:

En esta unidad, su niño aprenderá acerca de las matrices rectangulares y aprenderá cómo usar la suma para contar el número de objetos en una matriz. La matriz de abajo tiene 2 hileras y 3 columnas. Puede describirse así: 2 hileras con 3 fichas en cada columna, o 3 columnas con 2 fichas en cada columna.

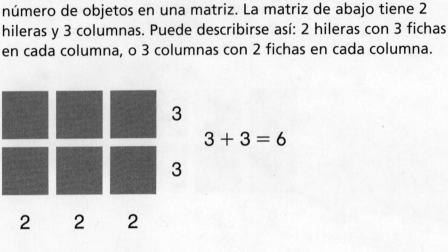

$$3 + 3 = 6$$

$$2 + 2 + 2 = 6$$

Usted puede ayudar a su niño practicando el uso de las palabras *matriz, hileras* y *columnas*. Por ejemplo, pídale que use monedas de un centavo u otros objetos pequeños para hacer una matriz que tenga 4 hileras con 5 objetos en cada una. Pida a su niño que escriba la ecuación de suma que muestra el número total de objetos en la matriz. ($5 + 5 + 5 + 5 = 20$ y $4 + 4 + 4 + 4 + 4 = 20$)

Su niño también aprenderá acerca de partes iguales de círculos y rectángulos: 2 *medios*, 3 *tercios* y 4 *cuartos*. Pueden practicar usando este vocabulario en casa. Por ejemplo: "Estoy cortando esta pizza en 4 cuartos".

Si tiene alguna duda o algún comentario, por favor comuníquese conmigo.

Atentamente,
El maestro de su niño

© Houghton Mifflin Harcourt Publishing Company

COMMON CORE

La Unidad 7 incluye los Common Core Standards for Mathematical Content for Operations and Algebraic Thinking 2.OA.1, 2.OA.3, 2.OA.4, Geometry 2.G.1, 2.G.2, 2.G.3, Measurement and Data 2.MD.5, 2.MD.6, and all Mathematical Practices.

Arrays, Partitioned Rectangles, and Equal Shares

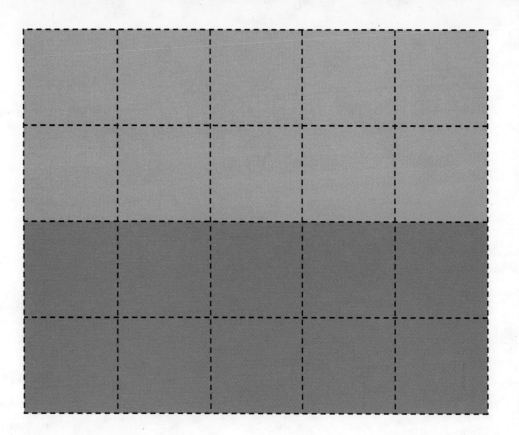

Name _____

► Shade Equal Shares

Measure in centimeters. Draw rows and columns.
Shade to show **halves**, **thirds**, and **fourths**.

10. halves   11. thirds   12. fourths

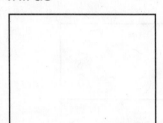

Measure in centimeters. Draw rows and columns.

13. Shade to show halves two different ways.

14. Shade to show fourths two different ways.

15. Shade to show halves two different ways.

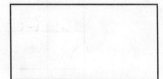   

VOCABULARY
equal shares

► More Practice with Partitions and Equal Shares

Measure in centimeters. Draw rows and columns.
Write the number of small squares.

16.

_____ squares

17.

_____ squares

18.

_____ squares

19.

_____ squares

20.

_____ squares

21.

_____ squares

Shade to show **equal shares**.

22. 2 halves

23. 3 thirds

24. 4 fourths

Find Equal Shares **305**

▶ Different Shapes of a Half of the Same Rectangle

1. Make two halves. Show different ways.
   Shade half of each rectangle.

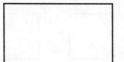   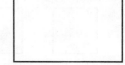

▶ Different Shapes of a Third of the Same Rectangle

2. Make three thirds. Show different ways.
   Shade a third of each rectangle.

  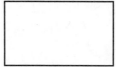 

▶ Different Shapes of a Fourth of the Same Rectangle

3. Make four fourths. Show different ways.
   Shade a fourth of each rectangle.

  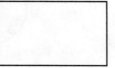 

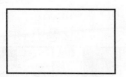 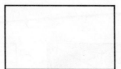  

► Equal Shares Using the Same Square

4. Make 2 equal shares. Show different ways. Shade half of each square.

□ □ □ □

5. Make 3 equal shares. Show different ways. Shade a third of each square.

□ □ □ □

6. Make 4 equal shares. Show different ways. Shade a fourth of each square.

□ □ □ □ □ □ □

► Equal Shares Using the Same Circle

7. Make 2 equal shares. Shade half of the circle.

○

8. Make 3 equal shares. Shade a third of the circle.

○

9. Make 4 equal shares. Shade a fourth of the circle.

○

► Different Shape but Same Size

10. Use Drawings 1, 2, and 3 to explain why the blue and yellow shares are equal.

1   2   3

▶ Solve and Discuss

Solve.   Show your work.

1. Carl draws a line segment that is 18 centimeters long.
   Then he makes it 14 centimeters longer. How long
   is the line segment now?

   ☐ _____
             unit

2. Samantha runs 45 meters, stops, and then she runs
   some more. She runs a total of 95 meters. How many
   meters does she run after her stop?

   ☐ _____
             unit

3. A ribbon is 48 inches long. Taylor uses 32 inches of
   the ribbon to make a bow. How much ribbon is left?

   ☐ _____
             unit

4. Mr. Parker cut 9 feet from the end of a pole. The pole
   is now 22 feet long. How long was the pole before
   Mr. Parker cut it?

   ☐ _____
             unit

▶ Solve and Discuss (continued)

Solve.   **Show your work.**

5. A race course is 99 meters long. There are trees
   along 38 meters of the course. How long is the part
   of the course without trees?

   [ ] _____
          unit

6. Michelle paints a fence that is 81 feet long. Huck
   paints a fence that is 56 feet long. How much longer
   is the fence Michelle paints?

   [ ] _____
          unit

7. O'Shanti has a necklace that is 24 centimeters long.
   She makes the necklace 36 centimeters longer.
   How long is the necklace now?

   [ ] _____
          unit

8. A giant flag is 6 meters long. Vern adds 4 meters to
   its length. How long is the flag now?

   [ ] _____
          unit

►Solve and Discuss (continued)

Solve.   **Show your work.**

9. Kelly has a piece of red yarn that is 25 centimeters
   long. She also has a piece of blue yarn that is
   11 centimeters long. How much longer is the red
   yarn than the blue yarn?

   ☐ _____
       unit

10. Paco swims 41 meters. Kenny swims 4 meters less
    than Paco. How far does Kenny swim?

    ☐ _____
        unit

11. Leonard walks 28 meters. Then he walks 56 more
    meters. How many meters does he walk in all?

    ☐ _____
        unit

12. A tree is 72 inches tall now. It is 12 inches taller
    than it was last year. How tall was the tree last year?

    ☐ _____
        unit

► Number Line Diagrams

Use the number line diagram to add or subtract.

---

13. Loop 17 and 28. Loop the difference *D*.

How long is it? _____

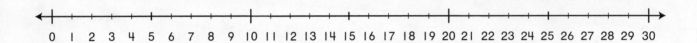

14. Loop 17 and 35. Loop the difference *D*.

How long is it? _____

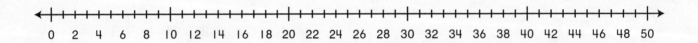

15. Loop 38 and 84. Loop the difference *D*.

How long is it? _____

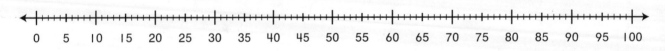

16. Loop 67. Add 26 to it. Loop the total *T*.

How long is it? _____

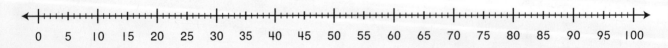

▶ Lengths at the Grocery Store

Choose a method to solve the problems. Does your method work for all of them? Be ready to explain your method to the class.

1. Someone breaks a jug of milk in the store. Mr. Green cleans it up. Then he blocks off the wet spot with tape. How long is the tape?

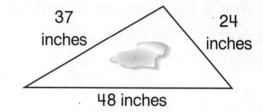

37 inches 24 inches

48 inches

```
┌──────────┐  _____
│          │      unit
└──────────┘
```

2. Mrs. Chang wants to decorate the table she uses for free food samples. She wants to put gold trim around the top of the table. How much trim will she need?

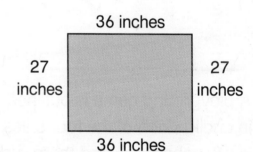

36 inches

27 inches 27 inches

36 inches

```
┌──────────┐  _____
│          │      unit
└──────────┘
```

3. Here is the route a customer takes while shopping at the store. How far does the customer walk altogether?

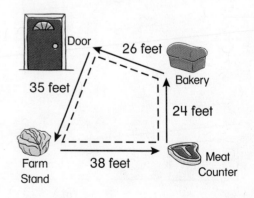

Door 26 feet

Bakery

35 feet 24 feet

Farm Stand 38 feet Meat Counter

```
┌──────────┐  _____
│          │      unit
└──────────┘
```

▶Playground Lengths

Solve.   Show your work.

---

4. The basketball court has sides that are 42 feet, 37 feet, 42 feet, and 37 feet and four right angles. What is the distance around the court?

☐ _____
  unit

5. The fence around the picnic area has sides with lengths of 33 yards, 56 yards, and 61 yards. What is the total length of the fence?

☐ _____
  unit

---

6. A playground game is outlined in chalk. Each of the four sides is 48 inches long and there are four right angles. What is the total length of the outline?

☐ _____
  unit

7. The sandbox has a wood border. The border has sides that are 32 feet, 45 feet, 29 feet, and 61 feet. What is distance around the sandbox?

☐ _____
  unit

▶Distance Around Shapes at Home

Solve.

Show your work.

---

8. A border outlines a flowerbed.
   How long is the border?

   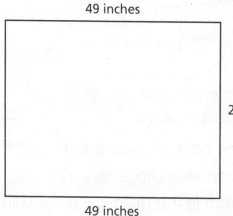

   55 inches

   29 inches   32 inches

   60 inches

   ☐ _____
         unit

---

9. The pantry has a tiled floor.
   What is the distance around
   the tiled floor?

   49 inches

   24 inches   24 inches

   49 inches

   ☐ _____
         unit

---

10. In spring, all of the wood floors
    get waxed. This part of the
    kitchen was waxed. What is the
    distance around the waxed part?

    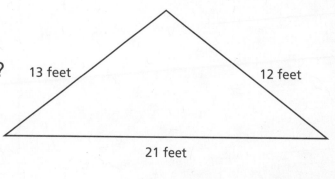

    13 feet   12 feet

    21 feet

    ☐ _____
          unit

Name _____

▶ Distance Around Shapes at School

Solve.   **Show your work.**

---

11. A picture hanging in the library
    has sides that are 39 inches,
    28 inches, 39 inches, and 28
    inches. What is the distance
    around the picture?

    ┌─────────┐
    │   │ _____
    └─────────┘   unit

12. The second grade makes an art
    project. The lengths of the sides
    of the project are 18 inches,
    24 inches, and 19 inches. The
    teacher wants to frame the
    project with tape. How much
    tape does she need?

    ┌─────────┐
    │   │ _____
    └─────────┘   unit

---

13. The cafeteria is a square room.
    Each side measures 47 feet.
    What is the distance around the
    room?

    ┌─────────┐
    │   │ _____
    └─────────┘   unit

14. The school patio has 4 sides.
    The lengths of the sides are
    22 feet, 18 feet, 27 feet, and
    16 feet. What is the distance
    around the patio?

    ┌─────────┐
    │   │ _____
    └─────────┘   unit

Add Three and Four Lengths

▶ Solve and Discuss

Solve.   **Show your work.**

---

1. Jorge is building shelves. The bottom shelf is
   64 inches long. The top shelf is 27 inches longer.
   How long is the top shelf?

   _____

---

2. The top of a bookcase is 24 inches from the ceiling.
   The ceiling is 96 inches tall. How tall is the bookcase?

   _____

---

3. Henry is putting a border of rocks around his garden.
   The lengths of the sides of the garden are 12 feet,
   19 feet, and 27 feet. How long will the border be?

   _____

---

4. Brendan is knitting a scarf. It is 28 centimeters long.
   Then he knits 18 centimeters more. How long is the
   scarf now?

   _____

▶ Length Word Problems

Solve.   Show your work.

---

5. Hannah has a red ribbon and a blue ribbon. The red ribbon is 17 cm long. The blue ribbon is 13 cm long. How much longer is the red ribbon than the blue ribbon?

_____

---

6. A roll of tape is 76 feet long to start. Karl uses 24 feet of the tape. How much tape is left?

_____

---

7. Nick and Ben are running a relay race. Nick runs 48 meters. Ben runs 37 meters. How many fewer meters does Ben run?

_____

---

8. Candace is putting a fence around her garden. The garden has 4 sides and 4 right angles. Each side of the garden is 23 feet long. How long will the fence be?

_____

▶ Length Word Problems

Solve.   Show your work.

9. Caroline uses tape to mark off the space where new grass was planted. The lengths of the sides of the space are 16 feet, 28 feet, 36 feet, and 18 feet. How much tape is needed?

_____

10. Lauren pulls the shade down. It covers 24 inches of the window. Jessica pulls it down 48 more inches. What is the length of the shade now?

_____

11. A flagpole is 62 feet tall. The flag covers 11 feet of the pole. How long is the part not covered by the flag?

_____

12. Miguel is putting a string of lights around a sign. The lengths of the sides of the sign are 26 inches, 18 inches, 26 inches, and 18 inches. What length of lights does he need?

_____

► **What's the Error?**

I'm trying to add 57 and 29. I'm not sure what to do next.

57 + 29 = ▢

[number line diagram: 0 5 10 15 20 25 30 35 40 45 50 55 60 65 70 75 80 85 90 95 100]

13. Show how to use the number line diagram to find the total.

57 + 29 = ▢

[number line diagram: 0 5 10 15 20 25 30 35 40 45 50 55 60 65 70 75 80 85 90 95 100]

► **Number Line Diagrams**

Represent each equation on the number line diagram.
Then find the difference or the total.

14. 43 + ▢ = 72

[number line diagram: 0 5 10 15 20 25 30 35 40 45 50 55 60 65 70 75 80 85 90 95 100]

15. ▢ + 28 = 86

[number line diagram: 0 5 10 15 20 25 30 35 40 45 50 55 60 65 70 75 80 85 90 95 100]

▶ Math and Flags

Ships can use flags to send messages.
A flag can be used alone to send a message.
A group of flags can be used to spell out
a message.

This flag means "I have a pilot on board."
It can also be used for the letter H.

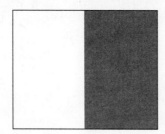

1. How many parts does the flag have?

   _____ parts

2. Does the flag show equal parts?

   yes   no

This flag means "Return to ship."
It can also be used for the letter P.

3. How many parts does the flag have?

   _____ parts

4. Does the flag show equal parts?

   yes   no

▶ Square Flags

5. Draw a square flag. Show halves. Color the flag. Color a half of the flag blue.

6. Draw a square flag. Show thirds. Color the flag. Color a third of the flag red.

▶ Rectangular Flags

7. Show 4 equal shares that are rectangles.

8. Show 4 equal shares that are triangles.

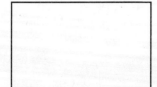 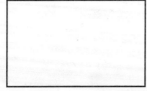

9. On a separate sheet of paper, design your own flag. Use equal parts. Color your flag.

Focus on Mathematical Practices

Write how many in each row and in each column.
Then write two addition equations for the array.

1. 🍎 🍎 🍎 _____
   🍎 🍎 🍎 _____
   🍎 🍎 🍎 _____
   🍎 🍎 🍎 _____

   ___ ___ ___

   _____

   _____

2.  _____

   _____

   ___ ___ ___

   _____

   _____

3. Measure in centimeters.
   Draw rows and columns. Write
   the number of small squares.

   _____ squares

4. Measure in inches.
   Draw rows and columns. Write
   the number of small squares.

   _____ squares

5. Shade half of
   the circle.

6. Shade a third of
   the circle.

7. Shade a fourth of
   the circle.

Show different ways.

8. Make two halves.

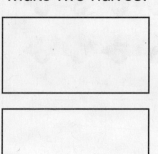

9. Make three thirds.

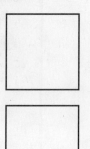

10. Make four fourths.

Show each equation on the number line diagram.
Then find the difference or the total.

11. 43 + ☐ = 62

|← |+++|+++|+++|+++|+++|+++|+++|+++|+++|+++|+++|+++|+++|+++|+++|+++|+++|+++|+++|+++| →|

0   5 10 15 20 25 30 35 40 45 50 55 60 65 70 75 80 85 90 95 100

12. 49 + 24 = ☐

|← |+++|+++|+++|+++|+++|+++|+++|+++|+++|+++|+++|+++|+++|+++|+++|+++|+++|+++|+++|+++| →|

0   5 10 15 20 25 30 35 40 45 50 55 60 65 70 75 80 85 90 95 100

13. ☐ + 36 = 81

|← |+++|+++|+++|+++|+++|+++|+++|+++|+++|+++|+++|+++|+++|+++|+++|+++|+++|+++|+++|+++| →|

0   5 10 15 20 25 30 35 40 45 50 55 60 65 70 75 80 85 90 95 100

Solve.   Show your work.

14. Amani has 42 inches of gold lace. She has 18 more
    inches of silver lace than gold lace. How many
    inches of silver lace does Amani have?

    ☐ _____
             unit

15. Nelson uses 16 inches of ribbon for each of three
    gifts he wraps. He uses 24 inches for the fourth gift.
    How many inches of ribbon does Nelson use in all?

    ☐ _____
             unit

16. The fence is 60 meters long. Dani has 24 more
    meters of the fence to paint. How many meters
    of the fence has she painted already?

    ☐ _____
             unit

17. Ymar has 22 meters of green fabric. She uses
    some of the fabric to make curtains. Now she has
    14 meters left. How many meters of fabric does
    Ymar use for curtains?

    ☐ _____
             unit

Solve.   **Show your work.**

18. Omar uses a blue ribbon around a square photo frame. Each side of the square is 16 centimeters long. How many centimeters of blue ribbon does Omar need?

```
┌─────┐   _____
│     │
└─────┘        unit
```

19. Malia puts a fence around her vegetable garden. The garden has 3 sides. One side is 12 feet. The second side is 15 feet long. The third side is 8 feet long. How many feet of fencing does Malia use?

```
┌─────┐   _____
│     │
└─────┘        unit
```

20. **Extended Response** Look at these shapes.

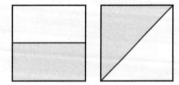

a. Are the shaded parts the same shape?

_____

_____

b. Are the shaded parts the same size?

_____

_____

Problem Types

	Result Unknown	Change Unknown	Start Unknown
Add To	Aisha has 46 stamps in her collection. Then her grandfather gives her 29 stamps. How many stamps does she have now? *Situation and Solution Equation[1]:* $46 + 29 = \square$	Aisha has 46 stamps in her collection. Then her grandfather gives her some stamps. Now she has 75 stamps. How many stamps did her grandfather give her? *Situation Equation:* $46 + \square = 75$ *Solution Equation:* $\square = 75 - 46$	Aisha has some stamps in her collection. Then her grandfather gives her 29 stamps. Now she has 75 stamps. How many stamps did she have to start? *Situation Equation:* $\square + 29 = 75$ *Solution Equation:* $\square = 75 - 29$
Take From	A store has 43 bottles of water at the start of the day. During the day, the store sells 25 bottles. How many bottles do they have at the end of the day? *Situation and Solution Equation:* $43 - 25 = \square$	A store has 43 bottles of water at the start of the day. The store has 18 bottles left at the end of the day. How many bottles does the store sell? *Situation Equation:* $43 - \square = 18$ *Solution Equation:* $\square = 43 - 18$	A store sells 25 bottles of water during one day. At the end of the day 18 bottles are left. How many bottles did the store have at the beginning of the day? *Situation Equation:* $\square - 25 = 18$ *Solution Equation:* $\square = 25 + 18$

[1] A situation equation represents the structure (action) in the problem situation. A solution equation shows the operation used to find the answer.

Problem Types continued

	Total Unknown	Addend Unknown	Both Addends Unknown
Put Together/ Take Apart	A clothing store has 39 shirts with short sleeves and 45 shirts with long sleeves. How many shirts does the store have in all?	Of the 84 shirts in a clothing store, 39 have short sleeves. The rest have long sleeves. How many shirts have long sleeves?	Pam has 24 roses. How many can she put in her red vase and how many in her blue vase?

Math Drawing[2]:

39   45

Situation and Solution Equation:
$39 + 45 = \square$

Math Drawing:

84

39

Situation Equation:
$84 = 39 + \square$

Solution Equation:
$84 - 39 = \square$

Math Drawing:

24

Situation Equation:
$24 = \square + \square$

[2]These math drawings are called Math Mountains in Grades 1–3 and break-apart drawings in Grades 4 and 5.

	Difference Unknown	Greater Unknown	Smaller Unknown
Compare[1]	Alex has 64 trading cards. Lucy has 48 trading cards. How many **more** trading cards does **Alex** have than Lucy? Lucy has 48 trading cards. Alex has 64 trading cards. How many **fewer** trading cards does **Lucy** have than Alex? *Math Drawing:* A [64] L [48] (?) *Situation Equation:* $48 + \square = 64$ or $\square = 64 - 48$ *Solution Equation:* $\square = 64 - 48$	**Leading Language** Lucy has 48 trading cards. Alex has 16 more trading cards than Lucy. How many trading cards does Alex have? **Misleading Language** Lucy has 48 trading cards. Lucy has 16 fewer trading cards than Alex. How many trading cards does Alex have? *Math Drawing:* A [?] L [48] (16) *Situation and Solution Equation:* $48 + 16 = \square$	**Leading Language** Alex has 64 trading cards. Lucy has 16 fewer trading cards than Alex. How many trading cards does Lucy have? **Misleading Language** Alex has 64 trading cards. Alex has 16 more trading cards than Lucy. How many trading cards does Lucy have? *Math Drawing:* A [64] L [?] (16) *Situation Equation:* $\square + 16 = 64$ or $\square = 64 - 16$ *Solution Equation:* $\square = 64 - 16$

[1]A comparison sentence can always be said in two ways. One way uses *more*, and the other uses *fewer* or *less*. Misleading language suggests the wrong operation. For example, it says *Lucy has 16 fewer trading cards than Alex*, but you have to add 16 cards to the number of cards Lucy has to get the number of cards Alex has.

Glossary

5-groups

| | | | | | | | | | | tens in 5-groups

○○○○○
○○○○○   ones in 5-groups

A

---

add

•••• ••

4 + 2 = 6

---

addend

5 + 6 = 11
↑   ↑
addends

Adding Up Method (for Subtraction)

144
− 68
‾‾‾‾
76

68 + 2 = 70
70 + 30 = 100
100 + 44 = 144
‾‾‾‾‾‾‾‾‾‾‾‾‾‾
76

---

addition doubles

Both addends (or partners) are the same.

4 + 4 = 8

A.M.

Use A.M. for times between midnight and noon.

---

analog clock

---

angle

These are angles.

---

array

This rectangular array has 3 rows and 5 columns.

bar graph

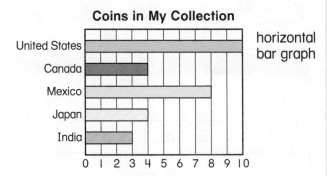

horizontal bar graph

vertical bar graph

break-apart

You can break apart a larger number to get two smaller amounts called break-aparts.

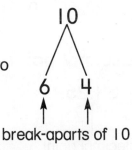

break-aparts of 10

cent

front   back

1 cent or 1¢ or $0.01

centimeter (cm)

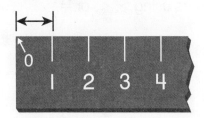

cent sign

56¢

↑

cent sign

clock

analog clock

digital clock

column

This rectangular array has 4 columns with 3 tiles in each column.

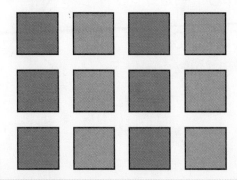

compare numbers

Compare numbers using >, <, or =.

52 > 25

25 < 52

25 = 25

comparison bars

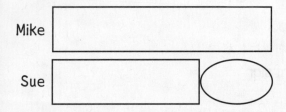

You can add labels and fill in numbers to help you solve *Compare* problems.

count all

$5 + 3 = \square$

1 2 3 4 5   6 7 8

• • • • • • • •

$5 + 3 = \boxed{8}$

count on

$5 + 3 = \boxed{8}$

$5 + \boxed{3} = 8$

$8 - 5 = \boxed{3}$

Already **5**

cube

D

data

	Sisters	Brothers
Kendra	2	1
Scott	2	0
Ida	0	1

← data

The data in the table show how many sisters and how many brothers each child has.

decade numbers

10, 20, 30, 40, 50, 60, 70, 80, 90

decimal point

$4.25

↑
decimal point

diagonal

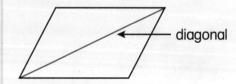

← diagonal

difference

$$11 - 3 = 8$$

$$
\begin{array}{r}
11 \\
-\ 3 \\
\hline
\text{difference} \longrightarrow 8
\end{array}
$$

digital clock

12:30

digits

0, 1, 2, 3, 4, 5, 6, 7, 8, 9

15 is a 2-digit number.

The 1 in 15 means 1 ten.

The 5 in 15 means 5 ones.

dime

front   back

10 cents or 10¢ or $0.10

dollar

 front

 back

100 cents or
100¢ or $1.00

dollar sign

$4.25

↑
dollar sign

doubles minus 1

7 + 7 = 14, so

7 + 6 = 13, 1 less than 14.

doubles minus 2

7 + 7 = 14, so

7 + 5 = 12, 2 less than 14.

doubles plus 1

6 + 6 = 12, so

6 + 7 = 13, 1 more than 12.

doubles plus 2

6 + 6 = 12, so

6 + 8 = 14, 2 more than 12.

E

equal shares

2 halves   4 fourths

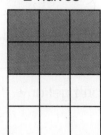   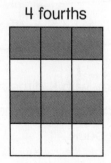

Glossary (continued)

equal to (=)

$$5 + 3 = 8$$

5 plus 3 is equal to 8.

equation

$$4 + 3 = 7 \qquad 7 = 4 + 3$$
$$9 - 5 = 4 \qquad 4 + 5 = 8 + 1$$

An equation must have an = sign.

equation chain

$$3 + 4 = 5 + 2 = 8 - 1 = 7$$

even number

A number is even if you can make groups of 2 and have none left over.

8 is an even number.

exact change

I will pay with 4 dimes and 3 pennies. That is the exact change. I won't get any money back.

expanded form

$$283 = 200 + 80 + 3$$

Expanded Method (for Addition)

$$
\begin{array}{r}
78 = 70 + 8 \\
+\,57 = 50 + 7 \\
\hline
120 + 15 = 135
\end{array}
$$

Expanded Method (for Subtraction)

$$
\begin{array}{r}
64 = \overset{50}{\cancel{60}} + \overset{14}{\cancel{4}} \\
-\,28 = 20 + 8 \\
\hline
30 + 6 = 36
\end{array}
$$

extra information

Franny has 8 kittens and 2 dogs. 4 kittens are asleep. How many kittens are awake?

$$8 - 4 = \boxed{4}$$

The number of dogs is extra information. It is not needed to solve the problem.

F

fewer

There are fewer ☐ than △.

© Houghton Mifflin Harcourt Publishing Company

foot (ft)

foot

12 inches = 1 foot   (not drawn to scale)

fourth

square

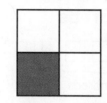

The picture shows 4 fourths. A fourth of the square is shaded.

G

greater than (>)

34   >   25

34 is greater than 25.

greatest

25   41   63

63 is the greatest number.

group name

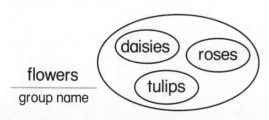

flowers
——————
group name

daisies roses tulips

H

half

square

The picture shows 2 halves. A half of the square is shaded.

half hour

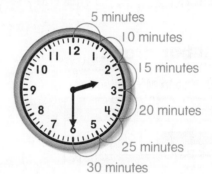

5 minutes
10 minutes
15 minutes
20 minutes
25 minutes
30 minutes

30 minutes = 1 half hour

hexagon

A hexagon has 6 sides and 6 angles.

hidden information

Heather bought a dozen eggs. She used 7 of them to make breakfast. How many eggs does she have left?

$$12 - 7 = \boxed{5}$$

The hidden information is that a dozen means 12.

horizontal

$$4 + 5 = 9$$

horizontal form   horizontal line

horizontal bar graph

Coins in My Collection

United States
Canada
Mexico
Japan
India

0 1 2 3 4 5 6 7 8 9 10

hour

60 minutes   5 minutes
55 minutes   10 minutes
50 minutes   15 minutes
45 minutes   20 minutes
40 minutes   25 minutes
35 minutes   30 minutes

60 minutes = 1 hour

hour hand

hour hand

hundreds

3 hundreds

347 has 3 hundreds.

hundreds

I

inch (in.)

1 inch

0   1   2

L

least

14   7   63

7 is the least number.

length

The length of the pencil is about 17 cm. (not to scale)

less than (<)

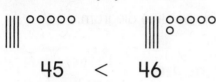

45 < 46

45 is less than 46.

line plot

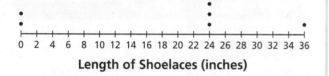

Length of Shoelaces (inches)

line segment

M

make a ten

8 + 6 = ☐

8 ●● | ●●●●

10 + 4
10 + 4 = 14,
so 8 + 6 = 14

matching drawing

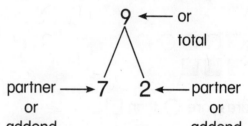

fewer

more

Math Mountain

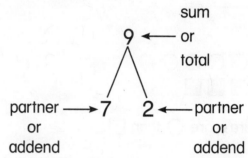

sum
or
total

partner → 7   2 ← partner
or   or
addend   addend

meter(m)

100 centimeters = 1 meter
(not drawn to scale)

minus

8 − 3 = 5

   8
 − 3
   5

8 minus 3 equals 5.

minute

1 minute

60 seconds = 1 minute

minute hand

minute hand: points to the minutes

more

There are more ◯ than ▢.

N

New Groups Above Method

$$
\begin{array}{r}
\overset{1}{56} \\
+\ 28 \\
\hline
84
\end{array}
$$

6 + 8 = 14
The 1 new ten in 14 goes up to the tens place.

New Groups Below Method

$$
\begin{array}{r}
56 \\
+\ 28 \\
\hline
\underset{1}{}84
\end{array}
$$

6 + 8 = 14
The 1 new ten in 14 goes below in the tens place.

nickel

front   back

5 cents or 5¢ or $0.05

---

not equal to (≠)

6 + 4 ≠ 8

6 + 4 is not equal to 8.

number line diagram

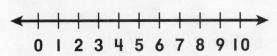

0 1 2 3 4 5 6 7 8 9 10

This is a number line diagram.

number name

12

twelve ⟵ number name

O

odd number

A number is odd if you can make groups of 2 and have one left over.

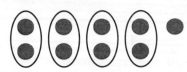

9 is an odd number.

ones

7 ones

347 has 7 ones.

ones

opposite operations

Addition and subtraction are opposite operations.

$$5 + 9 = 14$$
$$14 - 9 = 5$$

Use addition to check subtraction. Use subtraction to check addition.

opposite sides

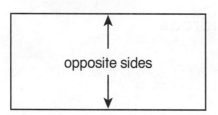

opposite sides

order

2, 5, 6

The numbers 2, 5, and 6 are in order from least to greatest.

P

pair

A group of 2 is a pair.

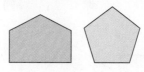

The picture shows 4 pairs of counters.

partner lengths

partner lengths of 4 cm

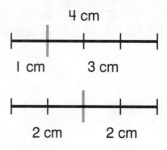

4 cm

1 cm   3 cm

2 cm   2 cm

partners

$$9 + 6 = 15$$

partners (addends)

penny

front   back

1 cent or 1¢ or $0.01

pentagon

A pentagon has 5 sides and 5 angles.

Glossary (continued)

picture graph

Flowers								
Vases								

plus

$3 + 2 = 5$

$$\begin{array}{r} 3 \\ + 2 \\ \hline 5 \end{array}$$

3 plus 2 equals 5.

P.M.

Use P.M. for times between noon and midnight.

proof drawing

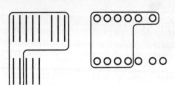

$86 + 57 = 143$

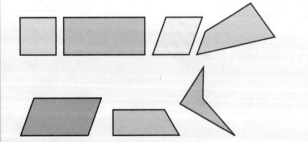
(label: Q)

quadrilateral

A quadrilateral has 4 sides and 4 angles.

quarter

front   back

25 cents or 25¢ or $0.25

A quarter is another name for a fourth.

A quarter is a fourth of a dollar.

quick hundreds

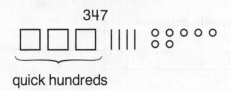

347

quick hundreds

quick tens

162

quick tens

(label: R)

rectangle

A rectangle has 4 sides and 4 right angles.
Opposite sides have the same length.

rectangular prism

right angle

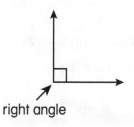

right angle

A right angle is sometimes called a *square corner*.

row

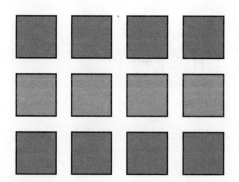

This rectangular array has 3 rows with 4 tiles in each row.

ruler

A ruler is used to measure length.

scale

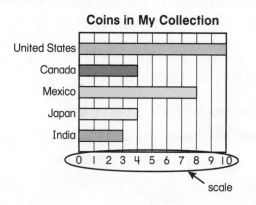

Coins in My Collection

scale

The numbers along the side or the bottom of a graph.

Show All Totals Method

```
   25          724
 + 48        + 158
 ----        -----
   60          800
   13           70
 ----           12
   73        -----
               882
```

situation equation

A baker baked 100 loaves of bread. He sold some loaves. There are 73 loaves left. How many loaves of bread did he sell?

$$100 - \square = 73$$

situation equation

skip count

skip count by 2s: 2, 4, 6, 8, . . .

skip count by 5s: 5, 10, 15, 20, . . .

skip count by 10s: 10, 20, 30, 40, 50, . . .

solution equation

A baker baked 100 loaves of bread. He sold some loaves. There are 73 loaves left. How many loaves of bread did he sell?

$100 - 73 = \boxed{}$

solution equation

square

A square has 4 equal sides and 4 right angles.

subtract

$8 - 5 = 3$

subtraction doubles

Both addends or partners are the same.

$8 - 4 = 4$

sum

$4 + 3 = 7$

$$\begin{array}{r} 4 \\ + 3 \\ \hline 7 \end{array}$$

sum ⟶

survey

When you collect data by asking people questions, you are taking a survey.

T

teen number

any number from 11 to 19

11 12 13 14 15 16 17 18 19

tens

4 tens

347 has 4 tens.

tens

third

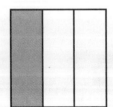

square

The picture shows 3 thirds. A third of the square is shaded.

thousand

1,000 = ten hundreds

total

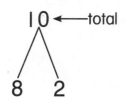

triangle

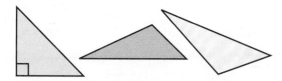

A triangle has 3 sides and 3 angles.

U

ungroup

Ungroup when you need more ones or tens to subtract.

Ungroup First Method

$$
\begin{array}{r}
6\,4 \\
-\,2\,8 \\
\hline
\end{array}
$$

↑ ↑
yes no

1. Check to see if there are enough tens and ones to subtract.

$$
\begin{array}{r}
{\scriptstyle 5\,14} \\
\cancel{6}\,\cancel{4} \\
-\,2\,8 \\
\hline
\end{array}
$$

2. You can get more ones by taking from the tens and putting them in the ones place.

$$
\begin{array}{r}
{\scriptstyle 5\,14} \\
\cancel{6}\,\cancel{4} \\
-\,2\,8 \\
\hline
3\,6
\end{array}
$$

3. Subtract from either right to left or left to right.

unknown addend

$$3 + \boxed{} = 9$$

↑
unknown addend

unknown total

$$3 + 6 = \boxed{}$$

↑
unknown total

V

vertical

$$
\begin{array}{r}
4 \\
+\,3 \\
\hline
7
\end{array}
$$

vertical form   vertical line

vertical bar graph

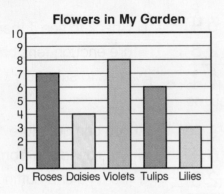

Flowers in My Garden

view

This is the side view of the rectangular prism above.

W

width

width or length

length width

Y

yard (yd)

3 feet = 1 yard (not drawn to scale)